VINO ARGENTINO

An Insider's Guide to the Wines and Wine Country of Argentina

By Laura Catena

Foreword by Jay Miller

Photographs by Sara Remington

CHRONICLE BOOKS

SAN FRANCISCO

Library of Congress Cataloging-in-Publication Data available.

ISBN 978-0-8118-7330-7

Manufactured in China.

Designed by Vanessa Dina.
Typesetting by DC Typography, Inc., San Francisco

Tango dancers on page 39:
Andrea Bonelli and Enzo De Lucca
andreabonelli@yahoo.com.ar

10 9 8 7 6 5 4 3 2 1

Chronicle Books LLC
680 Second Street
San Francisco, California 94107

www.chroniclebooks.com

To my husband, Daniel McDermott

Foreword 8

Introduction 10

15

CHAPTER I:
Argentine Wine Primer

34

CHAPTER II:
Argentine Food and the European
Immigrant Traditions

53

CHAPTER III:
Mendoza City: Gateway
to the Wine Country

65

CHAPTER IV:
El Este: Eastern Mendoza

77

CHAPTER V:
Primera Zona: Maipú and
Northern Luján de Cuyo

87

CHAPTER VI:
Luján de Cuyo: Perdriel

97

CHAPTER VII:
Luján de Cuyo: Agrelo
and Ugarteche

139

CHAPTER X:
Patagonia: Río Negro and
Neuquén Provinces

111

CHAPTER VIII:
The Uco Valley: Tupungato

149

CHAPTER XI:
Salta

127

CHAPTER IX:
The Southern Uco Valley: Tunuyán
and San Carlos

165

CHAPTER XII:
Touring Buenos Aires and the
Argentine Wine Country

Recipes 173

Wine Glossary 199

Bibliography 205

Contact Information 209

Maps 221

Acknowledgements 226

Index 228

Foreword

When famed wine critic Robert Parker asked me in 2006 to cover Argentina for his wine journal *Robert Parker's Wine Advocate*, I didn't know just how fortunate I was. As the owner of a retail wine shop in Baltimore's Harbor East from 2001 to 2006, I was vaguely aware that Argentina was becoming an increasingly important category, particularly in the range of wines under $20 a bottle, and that Malbec was the most significant varietal.

When I wrote my first review of Argentine wine for Parker in 2007, I ended up recommending more wines from that country than had been mentioned in the first twenty-eight years of his wine journal. It wasn't that Argentine wines had been the victim of benign neglect; it was simply a reflection of how suddenly they had become a major player in the import market. In 2008, Argentine exports to the United States increased by 33 percent in an otherwise down market. Today, Argentina sends about 35 percent of its total production to the States, although the Argentines consume more than three times as much wine per capita as we do here.

It's one thing to drink and enjoy the wine. It was not until I had made several trips to Argentina (both to the wine country and to Buenos Aires) that I began to acquire a deeper appreciation of just how significant Argentina's food and wine culture is to the experience. And this is where Laura Catena's book, *Vino Argentino*, enters the picture. Argentina has become an increasingly important destination for American tourists. More than 130,000 Americans currently reside in Buenos Aires, and many more are traveling there to visit Argentina's wine-producing regions, Mendoza in particular.

When I first visited, I thought that Mendoza, a province of over one million residents, was home to a single wine region, albeit a large one. It turns out that Mendoza has a number of subregions, and these do make a difference in what goes into the bottle. Laura also includes synopses of Salta and Patagonia, the two other important wine regions. The book does a superb job of describing the regions and the wines, but more importantly, it puts a human face on Argentina's wine country with profiles of influential wine personalities and recommendations for restaurants and other amenities. Argentina has a wonderful cuisine, perfect for the wines. Argentina's free-range beef is the best in the world, and there are many other regional specialties that Laura describes in both words and recipes.

How Laura had time to write this book is a mystery in itself. She is the mother of three young children and an emergency room physician in San Francisco; produces her own range of wines under the Luca label; works closely with her father, Nicolás Catena, at the Catena Zapata winery in Mendoza; and is a roving ambassador for the winery. Nevertheless, being the perfectionist that she obviously is, she has done a beautiful job. Anyone heading to Argentina, and particularly to wine country, should be carrying a copy of this terrific volume.

—Dr. Jay Miller,
wine critic, Robert Parker's Wine Advocate

Introduction

Argentina, the world's sixth largest producer of wine, is in the midst of a tourism boom, and wine is at its epicenter. In the last decade, many celebrated French winemakers have set up shop here. When I ask them why they have come to Argentina to make wine, they praise the *terroir*, the formidable Malbec grape, the altitude, and the accumulated word-of-mouth farming knowledge. Then, after a few drinks, they sheepishly admit that they are here because the people are such fun and the women are so beautiful.

Argentines live in the now, rarely thinking about the future, which historically has been anything but certain. They are deeply romantic and in love with nature, heading out to picnic in the mountains, to lie in the arms of a lover while sunbathing in a park, or to enjoy an *asado* (barbecue) at their favorite alfresco restaurant.

I was born in Mendoza, Argentina, *"la tierra del sol y del vino"*—"the land of sun and wine"—the province where that country's most famous wines are crafted. Mendoza is located on the westernmost border of Argentina and right in the country's midsection, a straight drive or flight west of Buenos Aires, the country's capital. (In Argentina, the name of each province and its capital city are one and the same. When an Argentine refers to Mendoza, he could be talking about the province or its capital city.)

In a country of romantics, Mendoza may be the most romantic place of all. It is a landscape of high drama, a vast desert region ringed by mountain peaks—"a place of almost supernatural beauty," in the words of the culinary historian Maricel Presilla. Rivers feed valleys that blossom into lush oases amid dry brush and desert. Living in these valleys, Mendozans envelop their homes in orchards and flowering vines. A drive through the countryside reveals porches entwined with fragrant jasmine, gardens scented with lavender, picture windows framed in eggplant-hued rhododendron blossoms, and sunny backyards filled with lemon and olive trees.

If ever there were a heaven for winemaking, Mendoza is it, with an enviable *terroir* (as the French call the environmental attributes of a place) of low-fertility soils, cool mountain nights, sunny days, and low humidity. In Mendoza, the nearby Andes Mountains function as a shelter from the Pacific rains and generate a microclimate of cool nights and the intense sunlight that comes with extreme high altitude—Mendoza is the only important wine region in the world with vineyards above three thousand feet in elevation. The well-drained alluvial soils—filled with rocks, pebbles, sand, lime, and clay—were formed millions of years ago by rivers and glaciers. Planting in these soils, which are less fertile than most, leads to naturally low yields of ripe and concentrated grapes—the secret to intense and age-worthy wines. Today, Mendoza has some fifteen hundred wineries.

Like many people who grew up in Mendoza, wine has defined my life. I belong to the fourth generation of an Argentinian-Italian winemaking family. Among the Catenas, a child's entrance into the world of young adulthood was marked by a sip of red wine mixed with soda at my grandfather's home. My great-grandfather founded the Catena winery in Mendoza in 1902 after emigrating from Italy. My father, Nicolás Catena, a third-generation winemaker, helped pioneer modern viticulture in Mendoza.

Today, our winery is internationally known for its highly rated vintages and for its role in pioneering Argentina's Malbec revolution. A grape varietal of French origin, Malbec was an important part of the blend of the famous Bordeaux *grands crus* in the 1700s and early 1800s. It has been widely planted in Argentina over the last century and a half, and in just the last decade, Malbec has become known around the world as Argentina's signature varietal and the source of its finest wines. It is appreciated for its dark color, rich black-fruit flavors, and smooth mouthfeel.

Vino Argentino is an insider's travelogue to the Argentine wine country. It is part viticultural primer, part cultural exploration, part introduction to the Argentine lifestyle. It is about the ascent of the mighty Malbec grape into the stratosphere of world-class wines. It is about single-lane roads lined with vineyards and patches of brush set against a breathtaking backdrop of snow-capped Andes peaks. It is about schoolchildren in white uniforms holding hands on dirt sidewalks, and gardens overflowing with flowers and fruit. In this book, I will take you exploring through the countryside of my childhood, so that you come to know its towns, vineyards, restaurants, and inns as intimately as I do.

Vino Argentino will lead you through the various wine regions of Mendoza, each with its own distinctive climate, soil, wine varietal, and social and viticultural history. You will understand why a Malbec from San Carlos is so different—blacker, more floral and more mineral—from the jammy and smooth old-vine Malbecs of Luján de Cuyo. You will long for the easygoing charms of Salta—even having your car blocked by cows standing in the road becomes an excuse to spend hours drinking *mate* with your fellow travelers. You will fantasize about the uninhabited plains of Patagonia, where aristocrats and Italian countesses have fallen in love with old vines and Pinot Noir. And

you will never again think of Argentine Malbec as the latest fashionable wine import; rather, you will long for the mountain-flanked vineyards of Mendoza, for the alfresco pleasures of a weekend *asado*, for the late-night dinners in Buenos Aires, for the old Mendozan wineries filled with nineteenth-century charm, and for the modern architectural creations of French wine industry scions. The recipes capture the textures and flavors of Argentine cookery, which is part Italian, part Spanish, and part Amerindian, but mostly about the national obsession with barbecued meats. This book is my personal invitation for you to visit and experience my country, Argentina.

Laura Catena

Chapter I:
ARGENTINE WINE PRIMER

The Early Days of Argentine Wine

Wine has long been an important part of Argentine food and culture, brought to the country mainly by immigrants from Italy and Spain in the late nineteenth and early twentieth centuries. Where many New World wine countries such as Chile, Australia, and New Zealand export most of their wine and drink very little at home, Argentines drink almost as much wine per capita as the Italians and the French. Don Antonio Pulenta, the ninety-year-old scion of the Pulenta family, told me, "When I was young, there were three kinds of drinks in the house: water, water with wine, and wine—and the amount of wine was determined by the age of the person."

Mendoza has always been at the epicenter of Argentine wine. In the eighteenth and early nineteenth centuries, Mendoza's agricultural products, which included wine, were transported by mules and carriages across the Andes to Santiago de Chile and through the pampas east to Buenos Aires. Once the railroad to Buenos Aires was finished in 1882, several years before those of Salta and the other wine-producing provinces, the dominance of Mendoza as a source of wine for the capital became inevitable. In the years that followed, Mendoza would become the number-one destination for the Spanish and Italian immigrants looking for a place to settle and apply their Old World winemaking knowledge. Mendoza became the location of Argentina's first vine nursery (the Quinta Nacional) and its first school of enology (Don Bosco). The climate and soils were ideal for viticulture—much more so than for raising cattle, which required heavy rains and fertile soils. Trained vineyard workers, winery products, and construction materials could be found with relative ease. The province and its population, largely of European descent, set out to sell Mendoza's wines in the heavily populated capital of Buenos Aires (up to this day, more than half the population of Argentina lives in Buenos Aires). During the 1960s and '70s, Argentina would become the fifth-largest producer of wine in the world and the sixth-largest consumer.

In Comes Nicolás Catena

Nicolás Catena is justly credited with putting Argentinean wines on the world map—by the best expedient of focusing entirely on quality. It's great to know he has started a wine dynasty, too.

—*Jancis Robinson,*
English wine expert and writer

The arrival of Argentinean wines on the world stage was initiated by Catena's vision and the way he changed the quality of wines for export, helped by his daughter. I have a deep admiration of him as visionary— a Mondavi in his own way.

—*Alfred Bonnie, DiamAndes Argentina and Château Malartic-Lagravière*

In the early 1980s, my father, Nicolás Catena, a third-generation Argentine of Italian descent, began a wine revolution in Mendoza. An economist by training, he was convinced that only by exporting world-class quality bottlings would Argentine wines have a chance at becoming an important player on the international wine scene. While taking a sabbatical in California, my father was inspired by the Napa Valley wine visionaries, especially Robert Mondavi. Having witnessed the Californians' determination to challenge Europe's iconic

Nicolás Catena

wines, he asked himself: *Why not try to do the same in Mendoza?* For almost a decade, my father studied the soils, the climate, the farming and winemaking practices of France, California, and our native Mendoza. He hired consultants from around the world: the Californian Paul Hobbs, France's Jacques Lurton, Italy's Attilio Pagli. His first conclusion was that only by planting at higher elevations, closer to the Andes, would he reach the cooler climates that were typical of the world's most renowned wine regions. Cooler climates allow the vines to ripen slowly, to retain acidity, to develop heightened aromas and complex flavors. He also found that our high-altitude desert climate had no equal in the rest of the world for growing wine grapes. So he mounted an in-house research department in order to study the intricacies of vine spacing, irrigation, and vineyard management and to develop the tools that would some day allow our region to produce a wine that could stand with the best of the world.

I joined the team as research director (while still practicing medicine) in the late 1990s, with a background in biology and medicine from Harvard and Stanford Universities. Needless to say, it was not easy to move from humans to plants. But just as in medicine, where the knowledge of an experienced physician is cherished above all else, I learned how to seek advice from older family members and experienced Argentine and foreign viticulturalists. Our discovery of the San Carlos area in the southern Uco Valley as the new promised land for Malbec in the 1990s was inspired by my grandfather Domingo's contention that San Carlos grapes make the darkest wines in Mendoza and by tasting the grapes of abandoned hundred-year-old vineyards in the region. The cool-climate, high-altitude movement sparked by my father has led Argentines to plant vines higher up—in the Andean foothills above four thousand feet in elevation—and farther south, where the climate is cooler (in Argentina, the seasons and the climates of north and south are reversed from that of the States). But the ancient collections of gorgeous Malbec, Torrontés, Bonarda, and Cabernet Sauvignon varietal rootstocks, all perfectly adapted to our climate, exist because of the multigenerational selection process they have undergone. And it is this historic understanding of our privileged Andean *terroir* that allows us to make profound and distinctive wines. The dry, cool, sunny high-altitude climate; the well-drained, not-too-fertile soils; and the spectacularly well-adapted Malbec grape combine to make a wine with bright, big-fruit aromas; rich, concentrated, silky tannins; and a sense of place—characteristics that are valued by wine drinkers around the world today.

The Land of Sun and Wine
The province of Mendoza makes 70 percent of the wine produced in Argentina, but the country has six other important wine-producing provinces, each with a rich history of its own. The wine-producing provinces of Argentina can be grouped into three regions: the Northwest (Salta, Catamarca, and La Rioja), Cuyo (Mendoza and San Juan), and Patagonia (Neuquén and Río Negro). They range from the northernmost Salta, at latitude 22 degrees south, to the southernmost Río Negro, at latitude 40 degrees south. The distance between

those two regions is 1,243 miles (2,000 km). Despite the distances they span, Argentina's viticultural regions share many climatic characteristics. All are located on the high plains near the mountains, and all have river-irrigated valleys, low-fertility desert soils, a relative scarcity of rain, and short-lived summer thunderstorms that wreak more fear than havoc on the vineyards. All also share the scourge of hail, which *can* wreak havoc on—and indeed destroy—a vineyard's entire crop.

Argentina is a country where every possible climate exists, from the northern jungles near Brazil and Paraguay to the eastern pampas, where fertile soils and abundant rain are nirvana to cows and horses. The south has glaciers and cold-loving animals (like penguins). In the west, the high-desert valleys at the base of the pre-Andean foothills are the golden land for viticulture. Because these are desert soils and therefore relatively infertile, grapevines are a natural crop. In low-fertility soils, grapevines tend to be naturally low yielding and have deeper root systems. The resulting wines are blessed with richer flavors and greater concentration.

A Little History

The history of Argentine winemaking is a story of immigrants and the rich traditions they brought to the New World. The story begins in Spanish colonial times, when Catholic priests who immigrated to the area with the conquistadors to convert the local Indians planted grapes to make sacramental wine.

It is thought that the Incas arrived in what is today Mendoza in the latter part of the fifteenth century and helped the local Huarpe Indians develop an irrigation system using the Andean snowmelt that flowed through the local rivers. The valley of Huentata, as Mendoza was called at the time, was at the southern border of the Incan empire called Tahuantinsuyo. Were it not for these Indian-made canals, the Spaniards would have encountered a much more arid and desert-like landscape when they arrived in the early part of the sixteenth century.

By the early seventeenth century, the Cuyo region was already famous for its wine production. The other main exports to Chile and Buenos Aires, transported by mule and wagon, were dried fruits, flower, olive oil, and distilled spirits. Until the late nineteenth century, Mendoza remained a small outpost. But that changed in 1882, when the Mendoza–Buenos Aires railroad was built and Buenos Aires became the indisputable central governing center. Argentina had gained independence from Spain in 1816, but the first few decades were fraught with regional battles between the Federalist *caudillos* (local warlords), who supported regional power, and the Unitarians, who sought to centralize power in the capital of Buenos Aires. Once the railroad was built, commerce between Mendoza and Chile came to a halt, and Mendoza became a major agricultural supplier to the other provinces, Buenos Aires, and the outside world, mainly Europe. The population of Mendoza exploded, attracting European immigrants, mostly from Italy and Spain. The European immigrants who came to Argentina in the late nineteenth and early twentieth centuries had the culture of wine in their blood. They brought the tradition of drinking wine with meals to the new land. In their small European villages of origin, people made their own wine or bought it from the few local wine producers. Homemade wine, called *vino patero*, is still sold along the backroads of Argentina today. Most Mendozans can tell you of a grandfather, an uncle, or someone else in the family who was and might still be making wine at home from grapes grown in their own backyard.

Prior to 1853, when the Quinta Nacional (the national vine nursery) was established in Mendoza, most of the vineyards in the region were planted with the Criolla grape, a pink, thick-skinned varietal that yields light and fruity rosé wines. Criolla is thought to have originated from the wild propagation of the original rootstocks brought by the Spanish priests and conquistadors in the sixteenth century. In 1853, the Frenchman Michel Aimé Pouget, founder of the Quinta Nacional vine nursery, brought a diversity of cuttings from France, including Malbec. Throughout the late 1800s and early 1900s, the Quinta Nacional was actively involved in bringing vine cuttings to Argentina, again mostly from France. In addition to a variety of Malbec cuttings, these included a selection of hundreds of common and rare European varietals, such as Alicante Bouchet, Gamay, Petit Verdot, Grenache Noir, Aspirant, Malvasia, Moscato, Pinot Noir, Semillón, Cabernet Sauvignon, and Cabernet Franc—all of which were planted at the Quinta for experimental purposes.

The first official records of vine plantings in Mendoza date to 1936 and were gathered by the Junta Reguladora de Bodegas y Vinos (Regulatory Junta for Wineries and Wines). These records show a total of 222,500 acres (90,000 hectares) under vine, with almost 60 percent of those being Malbec— 128,000 acres (51,775 hectares)—and other important ones being Petit Verdot, Bonarda, Criolla, Semillon, Cabernet Sauvignon, and Pinot Noir. I interviewed the late Rodolfo Reina Rutini—of the well-known Rutini family, founders of Bodega La Rural—in 2002 and asked him which varietals he remembered from the early twentieth century. "There was a lot of Malbec, which we called *la uva francesa* [the French grape]," he said, "and a red wine that we called

'Verdot,' which was very good, especially when blended with Malbec; there was also white Semillon of good quality in Luján de Cuyo and Maipú."

The first official records that exist at the I.N.V.—Instituto Nacional de Vitivinicultura (National Viticulture Institute)—which was founded in 1959, date to 1968. Out of an approximate 687,000 acres (278,000 hectares) of planted vineyards in all of Argentina, about 36 percent of the grapes were red, 21 percent were white, and 43 percent were pink Criolla. Malbec was responsible for almost half of the red varietal plantings, the rest being mostly Bonarda, Tempranillo, and Barbera. Today, there is almost no Barbera in Argentina, but a decent 25,000 acres (10,000 hectares) of Tempranillo remains. Bonarda, on the other hand, is now Argentina's second-most common red varietal. Among the whites, the most common varietal in the 1960s was the Pedro Giménez table grape, followed by Moscato d'Asti (almost nonexistent in the twenty-first century), Torrontés, Semillon, and Pinot Blanco. I find it interesting that there is no dominant Spanish or Italian varietal widely planted in Argentina today. Argentine Bonarda recently has been shown to be French Corbeau and not Italian Bonarda, and Argentine Torrontés is not related to the Spanish grape of the same name but is actually a native Argentine varietal. The six most common fine-wine varietals are all of French origin: Malbec, Bonarda, Cabernet Sauvignon, Syrah, Merlot, and Chardonnay. My friend Angel Paulucci, a grower who immigrated to Argentina from Italy in the 1940s, gave me his explanation: "You know, Señora Laura, I once tried to plant some Montepulciano here, in Tunuyán, because it grew so well in Abruzzo, where I am from. It was a big mistake, and I had to pull it all out, because nothing grows as well as Malbec in this region."

The second part of the twentieth century was one of turmoil: The country endured one economic crisis after another, along with a military dictatorship. Despite this, wine was still king at the lunch and dinner table, and brand names such as Escorihuela Gascón, Bianchi, Arizu, Luigi Bosca, Rutini, Saint Felicien, López, and Trapiche—all of which are still popular today—dominated the marketplace. Mendoza maintained a constant exchange of knowledge and technology with the still-existing Italian enology schools of Conigliano, Avellino, and Firenze. The Italian winemaking style of the 1950s was oxidative—meaning that wine was stored in large wooden casks with little temperature control. The resulting wines were rich in flavors, but lacked the varietal character and fresh-fruit aromas of wines that are available today and made in the protective style, which prevents excessive oxygen from coming into contact with the wines. Italy had its own wine revolution—at least a decade before Argentina did—wherein the oxidative style was put to rest, and such modern technologies as temperature control and stainless-steel tanks replaced some of the old ways. (Not all of the old ways were abandoned, however; in Italy today, some growers still bury their barrels underground as the Romans did centuries ago.) Up until the early 1960s, red wine blends dominated the Argentine table. Later on, in the 1960s and '70s, white and rosé wines became fashionable, and wineries adapted their styles to meet the trends of the day. Much as in the United States, Argentine producers used names such as Borgoña Tinto (Red Burgundy), copied from the famous regions in France, to qualify the style of their wine. It wasn't until the 1990s, that producers began to use varietal labeling to identify the grape of origin for each wine.

From 1950 to 1970, average wine consumption in Argentina increased from 66 to 92 liters per capita. At 100 liters per capita, Buenos Aires was behind only Paris and Rome in wine consumption. Very little wine was exported out of Argentina until the late 1990s, however. And it wasn't until 2002—following the devaluation of the Argentine peso—that exporting became substantially more profitable, leading to a marked rise in exports and the influx of foreign investors looking for opportunities to plant vineyards and make wine in Argentina. In the 1980s, my father, Nicolás Catena—a third-generation wine producer with a Ph.D. in economics—became determined to make world-class wines in Mendoza. Argentine winemakers knew that exporting could create an important new market for their wines, but few imagined that inroads could be made in the high-end sector. Restaurant wine lists and fine wine stores in the United States and Europe were dominated by French wines. California and Italy were slowly starting to see some success in the high-end sector; they had the advantage of a national cuisine with ubiquitous country-themed restaurants to support their wines. Argentine wine, on the other hand, had absolutely no name recognition on the international wine scene, and Argentine restaurants outside of Argentina were few and far between. I can remember that as late as 2000 the majority of sommeliers and wine buyers I encountered in my travels selling wine knew almost nothing about Argentine wine. Most Argentine producers looked at Chile's success in the low-end market and sought to emulate what our neighbors were doing.

My father realized that the entire wine culture, from the vineyard to the winery, had to be changed in order to produce premium wine in Mendoza. He set out to defy and challenge every notion that existed about viticulture in Argentina: the age of vines; the kind of plant material; the best altitude and latitude for planting Malbec, Chardonnay, and Cabernet Sauvignon grapes; irrigation methods; and winery methodologies. My father knew that South American wine was commonly perceived as inexpensive and inferior in quality, and that he could not export wine from Argentina unless it achieved world-class quality.

Argentina is a country where little bank credit exists, so investing in quality products and taking financial risks is only for the very daring or the very irresponsible, depending on your point of view. When my father took over the family business in the 1960s, the overproduction crisis was such that his father, Domingo, had to leave hundreds of acres of vines unharvested. Watching his father live through those harsh economic times made my father painfully aware of the chance he was about to take.

Malbec: The Black Wine

> I have a great memory of Robert Mondavi when he visited the Trapiche winery in 1994 and said to me "A great Malbec should impress through its attractive and deep purple color, its intense black fruit aromas with a hint of oak, and its sweet mouthfeel, soft as the bottom of a newborn baby..."
>
> —*Angel Mendoza, winemaker at Domaine St. Diego,*
> *and the "poet winemaker of Mendoza"*

Argentina's most famous wine grape varietal, Malbec, is perhaps the best suited to Mendoza's sunny mountain soil and climate. Malbec is one of the five Bordeaux varietals (the others are Merlot, Cabernet Sauvignon, Cabernet Franc, and Petit Verdot). Malbec is no fashionable flash in the pan, however; it combines the dark, ripe, concentrated flavors and aromas of its famous French siblings Cabernet Sauvignon and Syrah, with a richness and smoothness on the palate that has turned it into the fastest-growing wine import in the world. The dramatic increase in tourism to Argentina in the last few years will only serve to increase the popularity of Malbec.

Malbec: A Little History

> Malbec was originally a grape associated with southwest France, but
> today is much more glorious in South America.
> —*Jancis Robinson, English wine expert and writer*

The history of Argentine Malbec involves a nineteenth-century man named
Domingo Faustino Sarmiento, the soon-to-be president of Argentina, the man
who would become known as the father of Argentine education. Sarmiento
singlehandedly raised the literacy level throughout the country by creating
hundreds of rural schools. He admired the cultures of France and England for
what he considered their more civilized ways. (Ironically, the French later dealt
him a heavy hand when he tried to negotiate taxation and duties with them.)

In 1845, Sarmiento wrote a book called *Facundo*, in which he decried
the barbarian ways of Facundo Quiroga, a *caudillo* or regional "warlord"; the
caudillos ruled through fear and not law. Sarmiento wanted Argentina to
become a civilized nation and saw in the French and English models worth
pursuing.

At that time, the French were considered the world's undisputed
leaders of fine wine. In his effort to acquire the refined ways of France in
the mid-1800s, Sarmiento hired a Frenchman, Don Michel Aimé Pouget; to
establish a vine nursery in Mendoza. The Quinta Nacional, as the nursery
was known, was founded in 1853, two years before the 1855 Exposition of
Paris, when Napoleon III asked that a classification system for France's best
Bordeaux wines be established and displayed. The best wines were given the
title Premier Grand Cru Classé, and Lafite Rothschild, Haut-Brion, Latour,
Cheval Blanc, and Yquem made the cut. Three decades later, Sarmiento's
Quinta Nacional entered a Bordeaux blend (one we must assume was partly
composed of Malbec) in the Paris Exposition of 1889 and won a bronze medal.
Today, you can still see the legacy of classic French techniques in the tightly
spaced, low-rising plantings in a number of very old Argentine vineyards (such
as the Rosas vineyard in La Consulta).

The Quinta Nacional paved the way for the founding of the National
School of Agronomy, which became a driving force for viticultural and wine-
making education in Mendoza, under the leadership of Leopoldo Suarez.
This Argentina-born graduate of the famous Venetian winemaking school of
Conegliano brought dozens of new European varietals to Argentina, but none
of them ever became important enough to challenge the position of Malbec.

The famed English wine writer Hugh Johnson once told my father that before the late eighteenth century, Malbec appeared to have been the most important variety in parts of the Médoc, where most of the 1855 Classification wines came from. Other sources confirm that Malbec was widely planted in the St-Emilion area. A 1974 book—*La Seigneurie et le vignoble de Château Latour*, by Charles Higounet—quotes Lamothe, Château Latour's *régisseur* in 1807, as specifying that there were two noble varietals planted at the Château, Malbec and Cabernet Sauvignon. My friend Roberto de la Mota (winemaker at Weinert, Terrazas, and now at his own Mendel) tells me that he once met a certain Monsieur Jacques Herbrard (the owner by marriage and general manager of first-growth Château Cheval Blanc for much of the twentieth century), who told him that prior to the French phylloxera epidemic of the 1860s, Malbec represented sixty percent of the Château Cheval Blanc vineyard and of the entire St-Emilion area.

So you can imagine that when Michel Aimé Pouget brought Malbec and other cuttings to Mendoza from France in 1853, his aim was to establish an industry based on quality, defined at the time by what was planted in Bordeaux.

The late nineteenth and early twentieth centuries were a time of great promise for Argentina. The Argentines in power aspired to turn the nation, so blessed with natural riches, into one of the great countries of the world. Buenos Aires was heavily influenced by French architecture—beautiful stone buildings in neighborhoods like Recoleta are reminiscent of a similar period in Paris. In fact, Buenos Aires has so much French-style architecture that the city is often called "the Paris of South America."

Ironically, the Malbec grape, which was at the core of some of the greatest wines in Bordeaux, was decimated by phylloxera in its French homeland in the latter part of the nineteenth century—some 6.2 million acres (2.5 million hectares) of vines in France were destroyed by the disease, caused by an aphidlike insect, from 1875 to 1889. At the same time, in Argentina, the Malbec varietal was being widely planted and would lead its second home to winemaking fame more than one hundred years later.

In France, Malbec did not adapt well to the American rootstocks that were brought to Europe to save the vineyards from phylloxera. Because these rootstocks were more vigorous than the natural Malbec roots, the rootstock-grafted plants had excessive canopy growth, high yields, and grapes that had not ripened enough at the time of harvest. This was an important disadvantage in France, where rain and cold weather often force an early harvest. Later, during the big frost of 1956, the Bordelais Malbec was affected again, and this time, almost all of the Malbec in Bordeaux was replaced by Cabernet Sauvignon and Merlot.

At the time of the phylloxera epidemic in France, Malbec was being propagated throughout the province of Mendoza by new immigrants from Italy and Spain. The dry climate and sandy soils in Mendoza inhibited the propagation of phylloxera, and Malbec plants are almost never affected here. The grape ripens beautifully in Mendoza, where the growing season is long and the desert air is dry. Malbec was to become another successful European immigrant to Argentina.

The Immigrant Traditions

By the time my great-grandfather Nicolás Catena planted his first Malbec vines in Mendoza on the shores of the Tunuyán River in 1902, the railroad to Buenos Aires had been functioning for two decades and Mendoza had become an important trading partner with the capital of Argentina, Buenos Aires. The new immigrants planted vineyards and made wine—some in *damajuanas* (jugs), some in wooden barrels. My great-grandfather's first company, Bodegas y Viñedos Nicolás Catena, sold casks filled with blended wine to *négociant*-type bottling agents who would sell the wine in Buenos Aires and the provinces. Other families, such as the Rutinis, the Escorihuelas (Don Miguel Gascón), and the Benegas, bottled their own wines and sold them in the capital.

The early twentieth century saw the rise of an aristocracy that based its fortune primarily on the cattle industry, people who prized the fine wines of Mendoza. But it was mostly the immigrant Spaniards and Italians, accustomed to drinking the local wines daily in their home country, who continued these traditions in Argentina and generated a strong demand for local wines.

By the mid-1950s, with 120,000 acres (48,000 hectares) under vine, Malbec was the most widely planted fine red varietal in Mendoza. Argentina had become a real mecca for wine, and the Argentines drank it with enthusiasm. At that time, Argentina had more aging capacity in large wooden barrels than France. An Alsatian man in Nancy, France, Adolfo Fruhinshole, imported gigantic oak barrels, called "oak of Nancy," to Argentina. Those who bought hundreds of barrels won a prize: a sculpted barrel with the winery's logo. (You can see one of the original gift barrels at the Escorihuela Gascón winery in Godoy Cruz.) At this time, the domestic wine business was strong, and most foreign countries did not import large amounts of premium wines, so making an export wine business work was not financially feasible or even something that Argentines considered.

One financial crisis after another in the 1970s led to demand for value-priced wines in large volume in Argentina. This trend was followed by the "white and pink wine decades," when thousands of Malbec vines were pulled and Malbec plantings plummeted to 35,000 acres (14,000 hectares). Today, Malbec plantings are back up to 62,500 acres (25,000 hectares).

Malbec and the Quality Revolution

By 1980, my father had become concerned that wine was turning into a commodity and as such would have to compete merely on price with the other beverages that were becoming popular. So in 1981, our family moved to Berkeley, California, so that my father could take a sabbatical and work as a visiting agricultural economics professor at UC Berkeley. He continued to manage his wine business in Argentina from afar, selling fine wine from the family's Bodegas Esmeralda, a winery that produced the brand Saint Felicien, still well known in Argentina today.

For a winemaker, it was an inspiring, even thrilling time to be in California. The Californians were challenging the French hegemony on luxury wine, daring to compete with the best wines in France. In Napa Valley, my father learned of the 1976 Judgment of Paris, a competition in which Napa wines came out ahead of their counterparts in Burgundy and Bordeaux, and he began to think about making grand wines in Mendoza. After my parents moved back to Argentina, my father became obsessed with the quest for quality. He initially devoted most of his attention to Cabernet Sauvignon and Chardonnay, but my grandfather Domingo kept saying, "Nicolás, I have always told you that our Malbec can compete with the best wines of the world." So after several years of retraining and bringing back to health our old Angélica vineyard in Maipú, the quality of the juice being produced—its concentration, intense aromas, and rich tannins—was impossible to ignore. We started to put a great deal of energy into Malbec. From that came the extreme high-altitude plantings in Gualtallary, the development of a selection of high-quality Malbec cuttings—the Catena cuttings—the new plantings in San Carlos and Altamira, and the next two decades of redefining every aspect of Malbec winemaking and viticulture.

Alejandro Sejanovich

My father spent almost ten years studying the soils and climate of Mendoza. He reached the conclusion that the cool, high-altitude climate of Mendoza was ideal for quality viticulture. His Argentine team—head winemaker José Galante and viticulturalists Pedro Marchevsky and Alejandro Sejanovich—traveled around the globe learning every available vineyard technique and winery methodology.

But there were some areas that no consultant could help us with, and my father never blindly applied a methodology that worked in another part of the world without experimenting with it first in Argentina to make sure that it adapted to our climate. No other well-known wine region has vineyards as high in altitude or as low in fertility as ours, or depends on irrigation as much as we do. My father was the first to bring drip irrigation from Israel to Argentina. Dealing with high-altitude sunlight is another issue we continue to explore to this day.

The World Discovers Malbec

During the 1990s, the President Menem years, many public industries were privatized, and Argentines became enamored with democracy again. Because the dollar-to-peso bank-imposed exchange rate favored the peso, imports to Argentina grew tremendously and exports fell. Argentines traveled to North America and Europe as if they were neighboring countries. This also made our Argentine wines relatively expensive in the U.S. and European markets, and my father realized that unless he could sell wines above $15 in the ultra-premium category, he would not be able to make the business work.

The first real encouragement came from small retailers in the United States, who bought our Catena wines with gusto and vowed to promote them because of their high quality. Then came a great honor from *Wine Spectator* magazine: We were the first Argentine winery to be invited by the magazine to pour our wines at the 1995 New York Wine Experience, a tasting of the best wine estates in the world.

By the time my father released his 1994 Catena Malbec with kudos from Robert Parker, we were convinced as a company that Malbec could have a great future. In 1998, the 1996 Catena Alta Malbec was our first cuvée to receive ninety-four points on the one-hundred-point Robert Parker scale, and it drew the attention of wine enthusiasts around the world.

But it wasn't until the year 2002 that Malbec began to attract the attention of consumers worldwide—a result, no doubt, of the economic crisis of December 2001, which made the Argentine peso lose 65 percent of its value against the dollar. Since then, Argentines and foreigners have invested heavily in Argentine wine, and most of these projects are focused on quality. The foreigners involved (including the American Paul Hobbs, the French Michel Rolland, the Swiss Donald Hess, the Italian Alberto Antonini, and the Spanish José Manuel Ortega) have taken enormous care to train an entire generation of young Argentines and shown a great deal of respect for the Argentine *terroir* of Malbec.

Nicolás Catena: Malbec Pioneer

Nicolás Catena is a figure in Argentina of the stature of Robert Mondavi in Napa or Angelo Gaja in Piedmont. He inspired an entire region to strive for a higher level of quality by his successful exploration of high-altitude vineyards and rigorous clonal selection.

—Larry Stone, Master Sommelier and trustee, James Beard Foundation

In 2009, Nicolás Catena was the first South American to receive one of the highest honors in the world of wine: The English *Decanter Magazine* Man of the Year Award. *Decanter Magazine*'s chief editor, Sarah Kemp, confided that for the first time in the award's history (previous winners include Angelo Gaja and Robert Mondavi), the vote was unanimous.

In 1902, Nicolás's grandfather Nicola Catena, an immigrant from the Italian Marche region, planted his first Malbec vineyard in Mendoza. Today, Bodega Catena Zapata, the family's most prestigious property, is located in Agrelo, Luján de Cuyo. The bodega's wines—Nicolás Catena Zapata, Catena Zapata Adrianna Malbec, Catena Zapata Nicasia Malbec, Malbec Argentino, Catena Alta and Catena Cabernet Sauvignon, Malbec and Chardonnay—are sourced from five historic estate vineyards: Angélica, La Pirámide, Nicasia, Domingo, and Adrianna. Bodega Catena Zapata is the only South American winery selected by Robert Parker, Jr., as one of the top wine estates of the world in his book *The World's Greatest Wine Estates*.

My father is an extremely rational doctor of economics, a recluse, a dreamer, a passionate wine-lover, an extreme optimist (and pessimist), and a devoted husband and father.

When I was a teenager, my friends loved coming to our house and talking to my father about politics, history, music, art. He is the most intellectually curious person I have ever met. Interestingly, as he grows older, he becomes more open-minded and adventuresome—for him, every moment and every encounter is a learning opportunity.

When I was an undergraduate studying biology at Harvard, my father was throwing himself and everything he owned into making an Argentine wine that could compete with the best of the world. We would spend hours over dinner and a great bottle of wine, talking about plant physiology and experimentation, he telling me about what he was doing at the winery, and me expounding on molecular biology research. I knew very little about wine, other than what was in my blood from so many hours spent at the winery and vineyards as a child, yet my father would listen to my ideas and take my suggestions as if I had a Ph.D. in enology. It is this quality of always questioning, of wanting to learn, of never accepting something just because "it has always been that way" that has made him Argentina's wine-quality pioneer.

My father's mix of open-mindedness and determination has allowed him to do what no one thought was possible: bring Argentine wine to the forefront of the world of wine. But perhaps the single most important element that has driven my father is his true love of fine wine. When I began medical school

Laura Catena and Dante

at Stanford, he gave me an American Express credit card and told me to buy the best wines that I could find so that we could taste them together and learn from them. We would spend hours sampling Gaja, Vega Sicilia, Robert Mondavi, Château Lafite, and Domaine de la Romanée-Conti, and talking about the wines as if we might never be able to drink them again.

To this day, my father spends most of his time at the winery tasting and retasting the components and blends of Nicolás Catena Zapata Cabernet Sauvignon–Malbec, his favorite wine from our winery, to be sure the blend is right. I believe you can taste his spirit in this wine. (Zapata is my paternal grandmother's last name, and by Argentine tradition, it follows Catena—my paternal grandfather's last name—in my father's full name.) My father has created a community of winemakers and viticulturalists in Mendoza who believe that our region has extraordinary potential and that we should always strive to make the best wines in the world. These young people; my siblings, Ernesto and Adrianna; and I are the fortunate beneficiaries of the Nicolás Catena Zapata tradition.

The New Wave of Women Winemakers

In the late 1970s, Susana Balbo became one of the first women to graduate from Mendoza's Don Bosco School of Enology. Thirty years later, most Argentine wineries have women in all positions of winemaking and viticulture, from head winemaker (Estela Perinetti of Bodegas CARO) to owners of several of the best-known wineries: Susana Balbo (Dominio del Plata), Andrea Marchiori (partner at Viña Cobos), Catherine Péré-Vergé (Monteviejo), Annabelle Sielecki (Mendel), Sofia Pescarmona (Lagarde), and myself (Luca Winery), among others.

Each of these women has played a significant role in Argentina's wine history. Susana Balbo singlehandedly brought Torrontés back to life with her internationally popular Crios Torrontés, made in a much crisper, higher-acid style than was the norm. The flamenco-dancing, extreme-skier Estela Perinetti was the first Argentine woman to become chief winemaker of a major Mendozan winery, CARO, a partnership between Catena and Domaines Barons de Rothschild (Lafite), in 2000. Catherine Péré-Vergé has been the most actively involved owner among the Clos de los Siete French crew (aside from owner-winemaker Michel Rolland). Annabelle Sielecki teamed up with Roberto de la Mota to create Mendel, a winery that in just three years has become a major player at the high end in Argentine wine. Marina Gayan, who worked as head of exports for Catena for many years, became the first South American to receive the prestigious Master of Wine degree in 2003. More recently, Susana Balbo, head of Wines of Argentina, the country's main industry- and government-sponsored wine exports association for two terms in a row, has turned the organization into a serious tool for education about Argentine wine, with emphasis on the premium sector. Under Susana's tenure, Wines of Argentina has brought more journalists and wine competitions to Argentina from around the world than ever before.

Chapter II:
ARGENTINE FOOD AND
THE EUROPEAN IMMIGRANT
TRADITIONS

An Argentine Food Primer

Argentines live in two worlds: one rooted in the immigrant traditions of Italy and Spain, and the other a vibrant place with a thrilling sense of energy and change. It is said that Argentines have their feet planted in the Old World but their heads in the clouds; they're always dreaming up new things. A patent lawyer once told me that Argentines file more patents than anyone else in the world.

That sense of vibrant contrast carries over into mealtime. Mendozans have always had a strong family culture, and often prefer to eat at home or enjoy a simple barbecue at the Argentine equivalent of a taqueria. But the emergence of a cutting-edge and export-oriented wine community, along with the arrival of thousands of tourists, many of them food and wine aficionados, has engendered a true culinary revolution in Mendoza.

Much of that innovation has trickled in from Argentina's capital, Buenos Aires, which has a dedicated New York–style restaurant culture. In Buenos Aires, celebrity chefs routinely open venues and constantly dream up innovative concepts in food and ambiance. The most trendy and fashionable neighborhood in Buenos Aires is Palermo Viejo—recently subdivided into Palermo Soho and Palermo Hollywood. Only ten years ago, Palermo was a sleepy part of town filled with run-down European-style houses built in the early part of the twentieth century. Today, many of the neighborhood's grand old homes have been restored, and Palermo's vibrant community comprises dozens of cutting-edge restaurants, boutique hotels, and the latest in fashion and design.

The Argentine lifestyle straddles both the Old and the New Worlds. Argentines never go out to dinner before 11 P.M. in the summer, and habitually stay out with friends through the early hours of the morning. As tired as they might be from a late Saturday outing, however, they wouldn't dare skip their mother's Sunday family lunch (at our house, it's homemade ravioli with my mother's secret *pomodoro* sauce): It's a sacred tradition ingrained in a country where most people live and die in the same town where they were born.

In Argentina, meat has always been at the center of every meal. When I returned home on breaks from college in the States, my mother was always waiting for me with a *bifecito* (piece of flank steak) sizzling in the pan. That first *bifecito* after a long time abroad inevitably tasted better than any other.

Most Argentine beef is reared in the pampas, which includes parts of Buenos Aires, La Pampa, Córdoba, and Santa Fe Provinces. The secret of

Argentine beef is the grass-fed tranquility in which the animals are reared, which, according to chef Francis Mallmann, makes the meat more delicious. "They are less stressed," Mallmann says, " . . . there is no negative energy in their bodies." In fact, Argentine beef does not need to be aged to acquire the tender mouthfeel that we like in our beef, because the cows are slaughtered at a younger age and don't require all the fat that corn-fed animals need in order to have tender, juicy meat. Although Buenos Aires is the capital of beef, with such famous traditional eateries as La Brigada in San Telmo and Cabaña Las Lilas in Puerto Madero and La Dorita in Palermo, every Argentine town claims its own best place for *asado* (barbecue). In Mendoza City, that would be two places: Don Mario and La Barra. Mendoza, Salta, and Patagonia, Argentina's premium wine-producing regions, each have their own local specialties. Mendoza is known for its empanadas (meat turnovers), which are often made with chunks of meat rather than ground meat. Because olive trees grow abundantly in Mendoza and were planted in home gardens and vineyards by the Spanish and Italian immigrants, olives are a part of every appetizer dish and are used abundantly in the local empanada filling. Fruits are particularly sweet, ripe, and flavorful in Mendoza, so most people in the countryside make their own jams, preserves, and dried fruits to eat in winter.

In Salta, everything (including the aromatic Torrontés white wine varietal) is about spices and aromas. The classic empanadas of Salta are a bit spicy, with lots of onions and raisins (page 174). The *humitas* (corn in its husks) is made with red pepper flakes. Cumin is added to almost every dish. This spiciness is unusual for Argentina, where most people prefer their food not too spicy—the main flavorings being olive oil and garlic.

Patagonia is home to Argentina's best lamb and wild game—deer, duck, and wild rabbits—and the place where many Swiss and German immigrants settled. A typical meal at the famed Llao Llao Hotel in Bariloche, Patagonia, is a wild-meats charcuterie plate, followed by several versions of Gouda cheeses (fondue is an option) with wild berries on the side, then a large wooden platter of grilled venison and lamb, sautéed wild mushrooms, and garden potatoes. On the eastern Atlantic Coast of Patagonia there is an abundance of oysters, mussels, and king crab.

The Immigrants

In 1816, at the time of its independence from Spain, Argentina's population was five hundred thousand. Today it is forty million. At a little over one million square miles (1.6 million square km), Argentina is about 30 percent the size of the United States. Between 1856 and 1932, the years of the great European migration to the New World, 6.4 million Europeans immigrated to Argentina (to put it in perspective, 32 million immigrated to the United States at the same time and 5.2 million to Canada). Compare this number to the only one million Spaniards who actually relocated to the whole of the Americas during the three hundred years of Spanish rule. By the year 1914, 30 percent of the Argentine population had been born in Europe, and half the population of Buenos Aires was foreign born. From this historical fact comes the saying that "Mexicans descended from the Aztecs, Peruvians from the Incas, and Argentines from the ships."

The majority of these immigrants were Italian; in fact, by 1855, the Italians and the French outnumbered the Spaniards in Buenos Aires. Today, 60 percent of Argentines identify themselves as being of Italian descent. And from that comes an old joke (there are many jokes in South America about the arrogance of the Argentines): "An Argentine went to Italy and reported upon his return that he had been surprised to find that most people in Italy had Argentine last names."

Mendoza saw its fair share of Italian immigrants, generally young men who were involved in agriculture in their hometowns in Europe, among them my great-grandfather Nicola Catena. Nicola tended vines and orchards in the Marche region of Italy. There were also many immigrants from Spain, such as my great-grandfather on my mother's side, Emilio Zumel, from Valladolid, who met my great-grandmother María Napoli (from Genoa) in Rosario and then moved to Mendoza, where he sold vineyard fertilizers and equipment. Emilio had defied the typical pattern of the first generation marrying from the same origin after falling in love with my beautiful great-grandmother. She was Italian and, my mother tells me, quite defiant of traditions and social norms. Others, like Edward Norton, came to Argentina from England to help build the railroad, fell in love with their adoptive country, married an Argentine, and moved on to other industries—in Norton's case, to winemaking. Today the Norton winery is in the hands of Miguel Halstrick, who is nothing less than an Austrian turned Cuyano (what people from Mendoza are called). Needless to say, he does not like to be called Michael, his birth name, but Miguel.

The European immigrants of the late nineteenth and early twentieth centuries celebrated their good fortune in coming to Argentina with rituals that have endured through the generations. My father recalls watching his Italian grandfather Nicola eat a piece of steak every morning for breakfast as a reminder of his new home in the land of plenty. After Nicola became a successful vineyard owner in the early 1900s, he sailed to Italy and brought his parents back to Argentina with him. Sadly, Vincenzo and María Catena died less than two years after arriving in Mendoza, but Nicola always talked of how proud they had been to see "what an important man their youngest son had become." Despite living in this new generous land, the immigrants longed for their home countries and found ways to keep their native cultures alive. Nicola taught my grandfather Domingo Catena, his son, how to make prosciutto, canned olives, and tomatoes. My *nonno*—"grandfather" in Italian—kept his prosciuttos in a humid, mold-covered room under his house. Before dinner, Nonno would take my brother and me down the narrow stairs into this, his special room, to smell the aromas of cured ham and grab a few slices, which we would devour as fast as we could so that my mother wouldn't know that we were snacking before dinner. My great-grandmother María Napoli, aka Tita, taught my mother how to make gnocchi with pesto Genovese—a dish we still make every year for Christmas. Historian Samuel Baily of Rutgers University has written several books and articles on the European immigrants in South America. He explains why the Italian Argentines have such a strong group identity in their adopted country. One of the main differences between the Italians migrating to Argentina and those who went to the United States was that the latter arrived in the States a few decades after the English, the Irish, and the Germans, most of whom left Europe in the 1850s. The Italians were generally farmers with little industrial skills and a very different language. Argentina had a rapidly expanding wine industry, which was desperate to supply the masses of immigrants in Buenos Aires, and Mendoza needed men who could plant vineyards and make wine. The immigrants from wine-producing regions in Italy had greater skills and expertise in winemaking than the local Argentines.

The Italians who came to Argentina at the end of the nineteenth century and beginning of the twentieth found a large family network ready to receive them—such as the fellow Marche Italians who welcomed my great-grandfather Nicola in Rosario. My father tells me that when he started working for my grandfather in the 1960s, he asked Grandfather why a truck filled with produce, wine, and other goods was sent to Santa Fe province every year for Christmas. My grandfather said that this was a tradition established by Nicola, *his* father, who every year wanted to thank the Italian family who had first welcomed him to Argentina.

Every town in Argentina had an Italian Club: *el club italiano*. These clubs helped the immigrants find jobs, spouses, loans, and business connections. My great-grandfather Nicola Catena was the president of his local club.

Today, third-, fourth-, and fifth-generation Argentines of Spanish and Italian descent are receiving an influx of Europeans and North Americans who have come to Mendoza to build new wineries. It started with Jess Jackson in the 1990s, then the world-famous Michel Rolland, and then the Italians (Antonini, Pagli, and Cipresso), the French, the Spanish, and the Chileans who came in the late nineties and after the financial crisis of 2001. Forty-five percent of the wineries listed in a recent *Wine Advocate* review of Argentina are either owned by foreigners (fully or in part) or have a foreign wine consultant.

But we have to ask: What happened to all the Argentine Native peoples? After all, were it not for the Huarpe Indians, who built the elaborate canals that bring water from the Andes to the valleys of Mendoza's vineyards, there would be no viticulture today in Mendoza. The Argentine Indians—a small population of proud people accustomed to ruling their own lands—did not submit easily to the new Argentine government after independence from Spain. And the government did not make things easy on the native Argentines: Throughout the nineteenth century, three Argentine presidents, Rosas, Alsina, and Roca, led campaigns against the native Indians. In fact, Julio Argentino Roca, who was president for two terms in the latter part of the nineteenth century, was convinced that only by exterminating the Indians would Argentina be able to establish a peaceful, orderly civilization and open the door to brisk European immigration. Roca led the so-called Desert Campaigns in the 1870s, when thousands of Indians—men, women, and children—were killed. Today, although many Argentines have an Indian ancestor, most cannot trace their specific Native ancestry because of generations of intermarriage. The gaucho, symbol of the brave and fearless Argentine male, is usually of mixed Indian and European stock. The gaucho's riding and battle prowess is attributed to his Native heritage. In recent years, many things have changed in Argentina, among them the position of women (we have a female president, and women make up 45 percent of the workforce) and the view of our country's ethnic and historical identity. In 1985, much later than one would imagine, the Argentine congress passed the Law of Indigenous Rights, which gave legal status to all Amerindian communities within national territory. More people of Native descent live in the north of Argentina, due to the proximity to Peru and Paraguay and perhaps also because the local Natives of the north, the Guaraníes, were a warrior tribe that was never fully subdued by either the Spaniards or the Argentines. Patagonia has a large European ancestry because the local Natives, the Patagones and the Araucanos, had a very small population, and European immigrants were the first to actually inhabit most of this vast expanse of land.

A recent study by the University of Buenos Aires showed that 56 percent of the Argentine population has at least one Amerindian ancestor. In the last few decades, Argentines have become increasingly enamored of anything related to the Native Amerindian culture: the gaucho, *mate*-drinking customs, and the Native textiles and potteries of the north. Argentines have a newfound appreciation for the open land that is our country and that was inhabited for so many years by Native Amerindians.

The architecture of my family's winery, Catena Zapata, was inspired by the Mayan ruins of Central America and honors this ancient Native people. The Catena Zapata pyramid seeks to embody, through the Native Amerindian theme, the distinctive mountain *terroir* of Mendoza. Many Argentine wineries have used beautiful Indian names for their wines: Tikal, Kaiken, Melipal, Antucura, Amancaya, Chakana, Quara, Yacochuya, Tahuan, and Chacayes.

Our country is a true blend of cultures, where many different influences converge to create the modern Argentina. This mixture of ideologies, styles, and personalities is evident in our wines. You will find no two similar wines from Mendoza, but we all think we make the best wines in our country, and we all aspire to make the best wines in the world. The magic is in the mix.

Argentine Food Glossary

alfajores: A cookie sandwich usually made with two soft cookies held together by a layer of *dulce de leche. Alfajores* are often covered in chocolate or sprinkled with grated coconut. See recipe, page 192.

Argentine beef: Because it is grass-fed and slaughtered younger, Argentine beef is leaner, more tender, and gamier than other beefs around the world. The best-known cuts are *lomo* (tenderloin), *bife de chorizo* (similar to strip steak), *bife de costilla* (T-bone steak), and *cuadril* (sirloin, or entrecôte).

 I once took the famous Bostonian chef Todd English to my favorite local traditional *asado* lunch place in Buenos Aires. A few days before Todd's arrival, I went to the restaurant to warn them that I would be bringing a famous North American chef, and that Americans did not like their steak well done, which is how it's prepared in most Argentine restaurants—Argentine meat stays tender even when cooked well. The steak that they served him was indeed rare, so rare that he had to send it back. Todd politely suggested that I should let the chef cook the steak in the manner he was used to. I would give the same advice to you.

asado: Argentina's version of barbecue. A mixture of meat cuts is cooked over a slow fire for a couple of hours inside a cement or brick structure. Simple metal grill racks, either homemade or prefabricated, placed over an open fire are also popular. *Asado* meats can include various cuts of steak, ribs, Argentine chorizo, *morcilla* (black blood sausage), *mollejas* (sweetbreads), lamb, *chivito* (baby goat), chicken, and even an entire cow, goat, or pig. Most Argentines have a cement or brick *parrilla* (barbecue grill) in their backyard that they use every weekend. *Asado* meats are salted but rarely marinated prior to cooking.

carbonada: A meat stew usually cooked over an open fire. It's a dish commonly found in northern Argentina. The *carbonada* is generally comprised of square chunks of steak, goat, or lamb slowly cooked with onions, pumpkin, corn, and sometimes sliced peaches. Its level of spiciness depends on the region of origin. During the holidays, *carbonada* is often served inside a large carved-out baked pumpkin, making for a festive and decorative centerpiece. See recipe, page 178.

chimichurri: A chopped parsley, garlic, olive oil, and vinegar sauce that is served with steak and potatoes, and sometimes on top of chorizo. It can also be used as a marinade. See recipe, page 183.

choripán: Argentine chorizo served on a French bread bun. If you ask for mustard with your chorizo, prepare yourself to be quickly identified as a foreigner.

chorizo: Argentine chorizo is a local version of sweet Italian sausage made with pork, and is completely different from the spicy Spanish or Mexican sausages also called chorizo.

dulce de batata: A sweet potato "paste" similar to *dulce de membrillo*, or quince paste, but sweeter; best with cheese and walnuts.

dulce de leche: Milk and sugar cooked over low heat for hours until it reduces and caramelizes to a thick sauce. It is poured over flan (baked or steamed custard), or layered over thin pancakes (*panqueques*) or as a filling for the cookies called *alfajores*. See recipe, page 189.

dulce de membrillo: Quince paste, a molded Spanish sweet that is sliced and served with *cuartirolo*, a soft white cow's milk cheese, and sometimes locally grown walnuts for dessert.

empanadas: Turnovers filled with a mixture of ground meat cooked with onions, olives, and, depending on the province of origin, raisins. See recipe, page 174.

humitas: Cooked ground corn, onions, and lard wrapped in corn husks (*en chala*) and traditionally baked in a mud oven (*horno de barro*).

lomito: The small end of the tenderloin, or filet mignon, which is sliced and served in a sandwich by the same name.

lomo: Beef tenderloin, the leanest and finest cut.

mate: Yerba mate is a tea grown in the north of Argentina and Paraguay that is traditionally drunk hot out of a hollowed-out dried calabash gourd and through a metal straw called *bombilla*. It can be drunk sweet or dry, depending on one's preference. High in caffeine content and antioxidants, *mate* is often used as a pick-me-up in the morning or late afternoon. Sharing a *mate* while drinking from the same straw is a common friendship ritual in Argentina.

milanesa: Thinly sliced chicken or veal that is breaded and then fried or baked. A *la napolitana* is the version with ham and cheese on top. See recipe, page 181.

ojo de bife: Rib-eye steak, a favorite of Argentines; most restaurants will prepare it well done unless you ask for *jugoso* (juicy), which means rare.

parrilla: The metal grill on which Argentine *asado* (barbecue) is cooked; the word may also refer to the entire barbecue pit structure, as well as to a barbecue restaurant.

Chef Francis Mallmann and His Legacy

Francis Mallmann never stops reinventing himself and trying new experiences. He has been Argentina's most famous TV chef-personality; the co-owner (with Bodegas Escorihuela Gascón) of Mendoza's 1884 restaurant, the first fine-dining establishment in Mendoza (which opened in 1999); the owner of Patagonia Sur, the grungy La Boca neighborhood's own five-star restaurant in Buenos Aires; and most recently the author of Argentina's most celebrated cookbook: *Seven Fires: Grilling the Argentine Way* (Artisan, April 2009). But what I love most about Francis is his poetic way of looking at the world. Here is his answer to my question about food and wine pairing: "I accept that pairing exists, but I am against harmony in eating—I would rather have in my mouth two different glorious beasts fighting to convince me that they are the best rather than having the mellow melting of blending perfection that pushes me to a siesta. The edge of uncertainty—like walking on a cliff—that vertigo that invites us to go down and be part of nature."

An over-six-foot-tall, blond, blue-eyed Argentine of English descent who grew up in Patagonia and interned in famous Parisian kitchens at a young age, Francis Mallmann is fiercely proud of Argentina's traditional cuisine. His book, *Seven Fires*, is a celebration of the open-air barbecue, of Argentina's carnivorous culture, and of the virgin land of Patagonia where he grew up. Mallmann has been able to generate an international following for Argentine cuisine that is all about celebrating it and nothing about globalizing it; he is fearless about highlighting its unusual features (barbecuing a whole cow, say) and adding his own flavorful touches to traditional dishes—cooking empanadas with chunks of filet mignon rather than ground meat, for example.

Francis Mallmann has shown Argentina and the world that Argentine cuisine—our own European-influenced, barbecued-meat-dominated version of Latin American cookery—has a place at every carnivore's table, kitchen, and outdoor grill. Following is a recipe for a traditional Argentine *asado*, given to me by Mariano di Paola, winemaker at Rutini Winery and the designated *asador* (person responsible for the weekend *asado*) among his friends and family. Pay attention to the details, and you will understand the magic of Argentine barbecuing.

A Typical Argentine Asado

All Argentine *asados* (barbecues) begin with the meat selection, Mallmann's included. The most authentic *asados* feature a varied selection of cuts, as well as different sausages, including short ribs, flank roast, skirt steak, pork sausages, and blood sausages. About 1 pound (½ kg) of meat and sausages is the typical portion per adult.

Simple metal grill racks placed over an open fire are popular, as are built-in cement or brick structures. Because controlling the heat in different areas is all-important, most people prefer to use a movable grill rack that allows easy access to the wood. The first step is choosing the proper wood for the fire. A lighter wood such as cypress or pine will produce a lot of flames, but the embers won't last very long—perfect for a thinner piece of meat to be cooked rare. Denser, heavier hardwoods such as apple or oak take more time to light and have lower flames, but have longer-lasting embers for cooking larger cuts. If possible, a selection of both kinds of wood is best. The lighter woods will provide the first embers to begin the *asado*; the denser woods will provide longer-lasting embers for a nice finish. Calculate about 2 pounds (910 kg) of wood for each pound of meat.

It's important to always have a fire going off to the side of the grill—a "feeder fire" in a smaller barbecue grill—so you always have embers available to place under the grill and maintain the proper temperature. The best way to measure the temperature is to hold your hand 6 inches (15 cm) above the grill. If you can keep your hand there for 6 to 8 seconds, the fire is just right.

Once the fire is started, it's time to clean the grill grids. The grids should be left with the grease from the last cooking still on them—this ensures that they don't rust. Placing the grill rack over the flames of the lit fire will melt all the grease. After about 5 minutes, just wipe the grids clean with newspaper or a grill brush.

Now, it's time to season the meat. For a true Argentine barbecue, salt is the only necessary seasoning. It's important to use a medium- to large-grained sea salt or kosher salt. The larger grains absorb less liquid from the meat and keep it from drying out. In Argentina, it is said that using *sal gruesa* (coarse salt) perfectly salts each cut; the excess salt just falls off as you move the meat to the grill!

Place the cuts that take longest to grill—the short ribs and flank roast—on the grill rack. The short ribs should go on bone side down, and the flank roast should be placed fat side down.

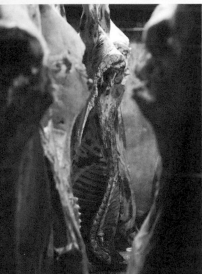

Add embers as necessary to keep the temperature at the proper level. Once you see a bit of juice coming out of the top of the meats, it's time to flip them over. At this time, put the skirt steak and chorizos (Italian sausage) on the grill; these only take about half the time to cook. Blood sausages, which are already cooked, go on last—you're just warming them up on the grill (be sure to turn them a time or two). Continue to cook for about 30 minutes for medium-rare meat, 35 minutes for medium, and 40 minutes for medium-well.

Chapter III:
MENDOZA CITY:
GATEWAY TO THE
WINE COUNTRY

MENDOZA CITY At a Glance

VINO — MAR 10 30 PM 1922 — TRAVEL

Getting There: Mendoza City is a half-hour plane ride from Santiago de Chile across the Andes and a 90-minute flight from Argentina's capital, Buenos Aires.

Where to Go: The city's squares, pedestrian promenade, and late-night restaurants. The nearest wineries are far enough from the center of town that you will need a taxi to reach them.

Wines/Varietals: These restaurants have the most comprehensive wine lists: Azafrán (you can peruse the cellar to pick your wine), Bistro M (in the Park Hyatt hotel), Francesco Ristorante, the Vines of Mendoza Tasting Room, and Mallmann's 1884.

Food: Argentine asado, fresh salads made with locally grown produce, homemade pastas.

Climate: Mendoza City is warmer than the adjoining wine country because of its lower altitude, so you can enjoy dining alfresco throughout the spring, summer, and fall.

Leisurely Argentina

With its shady, sycamore-lined streets; spacious, open-air plazas; and outdoor cafes, downtown Mendoza is the perfect place to take a leisurely stroll, stop for an espresso, and enjoy the city well into the night. This captivating Spanish colonial city has a laidback provincial feel, essentially shutting down every day from 2 to 4 P.M., when people head home for lunch and a siesta. Mendozans are very proud of their city and its cleanliness; you won't find better-kept sidewalks (or less dog poop) anywhere else in Argentina. Mendoza has a well-organized system of buses and trolleys that can take you almost anywhere in the city.

Although Mendoza has all the amenities of a metropolitan city, it feels more like a village than its sister city, the cosmopolitan Argentine capital, Buenos Aires. Much of Mendoza City is an old colonial town, dotted with beautiful squares—Plaza Chile, Plaza Italia, Plaza España, Plaza San Martín, and Plaza Independencia—and a centrally located park, Parque General San Martín, filled with drink vendors, joggers and bikers, picnickers, a merry-go-round, a zoo, and even a tall hill (Cerro de la Gloria), which has a panoramic view of the city. Across the main square (Plaza Independencia) is a pedestrian promenade with cafes, ice cream stores, shops, and abundant outdoor seating, the perfect place to people-watch. On Sunday, the main square is filled with street vendors offering handmade leather sandals and bags, wooden instruments, *mate* gourds and straws, and all kinds of artisanal goods.

A Little History

The founding fathers of Mendoza Province were a group of Spanish Chilean *encomenderos*—Spanish colonists given the rights to land in exchange for taxes—who crossed over from Chile and spent several decades ruling their Mendozan lands from their Chilean homes. For its first 216 years, the province of Cuyo and the city of Mendoza belonged to the "Capitancy of Chile," and not to what was later to become the Argentine Territory, governed from the capital of Buenos Aires.

The city of Mendoza was founded in 1561, three decades before the founding of Buenos Aires. The city was established by a Spanish captain named Pedro del Castillo, sent here from Peru through Chile and over the Andes. Captain Castillo named the city in honor of the Chilean governor at the time, Don Garcia Hurtado de Mendoza. A 1571 chronicle by a certain Don Juan Lopez de Velazco cites that there were "150 Spanish settlers in Mendoza . . . and there are 4,000 tributary Indians . . . there is valley territory where a certain type of fig, corn, barley, and grapevines grow on irrigated land, providing supplies to the Spanish as far away as Santiago, Chile." This is the first documentation of vines in Mendoza.

Agricultural crops propagated rapidly in Mendoza, thanks to the wide network of canals stretching for hundreds of kilometers from the Andes, the handiwork of the local Huarpe Indians who cultivated potatoes and corn in these irrigated Mendozan valleys during the fifteenth and sixteenth centuries. The culture of the Huarpe Indians was rooted in farming, not war. By 1595, so much wine was being made (mostly by priests) in Cuyo and the neighboring provinces that the Spanish king prohibited the further production of wine in the region, fearing that it would compete with the Spanish wine industry. The only real effect of this law was that plants were left to grow wild and propagate through seeds rather than canes, resulting in a wild kind of grapevine called Criolla that still exists throughout the region and is used to make light, inexpensive rosé wines. But wine consumption remained strong, and home winemaking became a household custom, no different from owning a few head of cattle or growing a vegetable garden.

By the early seventeenth century, the Cuyo region (which includes Mendoza Province and the bordering provinces of San Juan and San Luis— though only Mendoza and San Juan are important for wine) had become famous for its wine production. For the next two centuries, Mendozan wines were transported to Chile and Buenos Aires in clay containers carried by donkeys or in wooden carriages covered with leather or straw. In fact, it wasn't until the 1800s that these clay pots were replaced by wooden casks brought to Argentina by Spanish and Italian immigrants.

Still, throughout the seventeenth century, Mendoza remained a small outpost, mostly dependent on a few colonists. During this time, Salta, the capital of Salta Province, was a much more important city than Mendoza. Located closer to Peru and the silver mines of Potosí, Salta had a vibrant commerce in food, clothing, and goods needed by the Indians who worked the mines.

But all that changed in 1882, when the Mendoza–Buenos Aires railroad was built. Buenos Aires had become the undisputable central governing center, and when the railway was finished, commerce between Mendoza and Chile stopped almost completely. Mendoza became a mainstay of agricultural supplies to Buenos Aires and to the outside world, mainly Europe. The population of Mendoza grew by leaps and bounds, attracting a multitude of European immigrants. Today, with its population of 850,000, greater Mendoza is the fourth-largest metropolitan area in Argentina.

The second part of the nineteenth century was a crucial period for the wine industry in Mendoza. At the time, Argentina was ruled by an intellectual group of Francophiles (which included President Sarmiento), who based their ideas of "Argentinism" on a society that embraced the enlightened romanticism of nineteenth-century France. Buenos Aires is littered with the architectural remnants of the country's late-nineteenth- and early-twentieth-century love affair with France. And although Mendoza has fewer relics from this architectural period, it does have a legacy of several thousand hectares of vines, many originating from this period.

Chin Chin! Mendoza's Annual Celebrations

A perfect way to experience Mendoza is by attending one of the city's annual celebrations. One event in particular showcases the city's provincial heart: Mendoza's annual grape harvest celebration, La Fiesta de la Vendimia, an elaborate folklore show and beauty pageant that dates back to 1913. One of its biggest events is the competition for the title of Reina de la Vendimia (Queen of the Harvest). The winner is crowned in the Teatro Griego, a gigantic amphitheater where dancers dressed in every imaginable form of traditional wear create a spectacular show. The photo of the winning queen makes the front cover of every newspaper the following day, and intense debates arise in every office, cafe, and family on whether the winning queen is truly the fairest of them all. The beauty pageant is taken (almost) as seriously as the World Soccer Cup, and certainly more seriously than the local elections. Argentines love their traditions and their beautiful women.

The Masters of Food and Wine event is an upscale wine and food celebration held annually at the end of February. It was started in 2006 by the former general manager of the Park Hyatt Mendoza, Carl Emberson, and attracts hundreds of wine-lovers and celebrity chefs from around the world. The events include wine tastings and meals all around Mendoza and Buenos Aires.

Las Acequias: Why Mendoza Has Trees

Guidebooks on Mendoza warn you of the *acequias* (open ditches) that line every street and sidewalk. Distracted walkers and tourists have been known to break a leg by falling into an *acequia*. In fact, to get into a car parked on a street in Mendoza, you have to go over a little bridge and then tip-toe around to open the door. *Acequias* carry the runoff water from the Andes snowmelt as well as rain and irrigation water. Without it, the trees that line each and every street in Mendoza would not survive the high-desert climate. Our gorgeous city would show an entirely different face.

The original ditches were extensions of the irrigation canals established by the Huarpe Indians to farm the land. In the 1870s, a group of tree-obsessed Mendozan City officials built an elaborate open-air canal system that carried runoff water next to every sidewalk and gave life to the city's trees. *Acequias* were placed on every street in Mendoza. European immigrants embraced this local custom wholeheartedly, because the tree-planted boulevards and avenues reminded them of their native Europe. This love of trees is passed on from generation to generation. My grandfather planted the 165 elm trees that line the avenue of our country home at La Vendimia, and it is the job of my children and their cousins to make sure that these trees are well cared for during their lifetime.

The Five Plazas

After Mendoza City was decimated by an earthquake in 1861—four thousand people lost their lives, and most of the city's buildings were reduced to rubble—five wide, spacious plazas were constructed. The idea was that if another earthquake struck, the citizens would have an open place in which to take refuge. The plazas represent the major historical and cultural influences on the city. Each of the five plazas is equidistant to the central square. The largest, Plaza Independencia, stands between the colonial-style Park Hyatt hotel and the walking promenade, Peatonal Sarmiento, which is lined with ice cream shops and outdoor cafes. On weekends, the Plaza Independencia hosts an artisanal fair and often features live music. The Museum of Modern Art is located in an underground area below the plaza.

Set in the middle of the city's financial district, the Plaza San Martín holds a gigantic statue of the *Libertador* ("Liberator"), General San Martín, the man who led the troops that defeated the Spaniards in Argentina's war for independence, which lasted from 1810 to 1816. His poetic/patriotic name is San Martín de los Andes (Saint Martín of the Andes), and every Mendozan derives a certain pride from the fact that Argentina's general liberator was once governor of Mendoza Province.

Plaza Chile, with its spectacular giant pepper tree and the best children's playground in the city, was built to honor the close connection Mendoza has with its neighboring country Chile. The square was named in appreciation of the relief and support that Chile gave Mendoza after the devastating earthquake of 1861. The plaza has a central statue of San Martín and Bernardo O'Higgins (the Chilean liberator) holding a sword with joined hands. The two generals, who were close friends, joined forces to fight the Spaniards in the early 1800s. Although Chileans and Mendozans like to joke about their winemaking rivalry, the adjacent states and their citizens share a close affinity. In fact, four of Argentina's leading wineries belong to Chilean companies: Kaiken (Aurelio Montes), Trivento (Concha y Toro), Doña Paula (Santa Rita), and Renacer (Reich family).

The Italian immigrants who arrived in the region in the nineteenth century had a profound influence on Mendoza, and Plaza Italia was built in their honor. The square has a rendering of the famous statue of the she-wolf suckling Romulus and Remus—the symbol of Rome—and a central fountain with fourteen hundred ceramic tiles inspired by the San Petronio Cathedral of Bologna. The Festa in Piazza that occurs annually in late February is an entertaining Italian festival held at the plaza.

My favorite of the five squares is Plaza España; the central fountain is reminiscent of an old Spanish patio. The plaza was remodeled in 1946 with new tiles brought from Spain. Its art tells the story of how the city of Mendoza was founded in 1561.

Mendoza City Wineries
Bodegas Escorihuela Gascón and Mallmann's 1884
Bodegas Escorihuela Gascón is the oldest winery still in operation in Mendoza City (it is located in the Godoy Cruz neighborhood, a ten-minute drive from Plaza Independencia). It was founded in 1884 by Don Miguel Gascón, who immigrated to Argentina from Aragón, Spain, in 1880. Don Miguel became famous in Mendoza in 1920 when he built Mendoza's highest building at the time—nine stories tall—and decorated it with stained glass imported from France. A year after its inauguration, an earthquake decimated the area but left the building intact.

Don Miguel was a Francophile who traveled regularly to France to acquire winemaking know-how and culture. He became one of the biggest importers of large French oak barrels to Argentina and named his best wines after French places or foods: Carcassonne for his most popular table wine, and Pont l'Evêque (a cheese) for his *tête de cuvée* (most prestigious wine), the pure Malbec that was to become President Perón's favorite wine in the 1940s. To this day, the two brands remain well known in Argentina.

On the premises is Francis Mallmann's celebrated restaurant, 1884, which opened in 1999, the first restaurant within a winery in Mendoza. The restaurant is a required stop for any wine- and food-lover visiting Mendoza. Mallmann's 1884 is filled with a lively mix of locals and tourists. They come to watch empanadas and *humitas* come out of the outdoor mud oven; to eat colorful green salads dressed with tomatoes that have been sun-dried in the restaurant's garden; to taste breads made with whole grains and seeds and baked in the outdoor oven; to sample empanadas filled with sliced onions, olives, and pieces of tender meat; and to enjoy the creamy, nutty flavors of grilled *provoleta* cheese sprinkled with locally grown oregano. The wine list has an impressive collection of Argentine wines.

Bodegas CARO: The Marriage of Two Varietals

In the 1980s, when my father started his ambitious project to reshape the future of Argentine wine, he never dreamed that one day he would be partnering with the owners of first-growth Château Lafite Rothschild to make a wine in Argentina. In 1999, a mutual friend, Jim Galtieri, had convinced Eric de Rothschild and general manager Christophe Salin to visit Mendoza on their way back from Chile. My father prepared a tasting of Catena Cabernet Sauvignon and Malbec dating to the early 1990s. It was the beginning of a friendship and partnership between two families and two varietals: the Rothschilds and the Catenas, the Cabernet Sauvignon and the Malbec. Initially, the Rothschild team was more excited about Cabernet Sauvignon than Malbec, but winemaker Estela Perinetti's ability to find fabulous old-vine sources of both varietals has made the blend more balanced over the years, with a fifty-fifty breakdown as of late.

In 2002, the CARO partnership of Catena and Rothschild (established in 1999) purchased a part of the old Escorihuela winery and built its own winemaking facility there, employing state-of-the-art technology in a beautiful old-brick Italian Renaissance–style building that dates back to the nineteenth century. The full renovation should be finished by late 2010, when the ancient

Estela Perinetti

underground caves and indoor patios of CARO will be open to the public. CARO, which means "dear" in Italian, combines the names Catena and Rothschild in a project that is indeed dear to all involved. In fact, Baron Eric admits that when he starts sipping CARO wine, he can't stop because it's so smooth and easy to drink.

Chapter IV:
EL ESTE:
EASTERN MENDOZA

EL ESTE At a Glance

Getting There: Take the Ruta 7 east of Mendoza City and drive for 30 minutes to 1 hour.

Where to Go: Wineries and small villages.

Wines/Varietals: Bonarda, Tempranillo, Syrah, and Petit Verdot.

Food: Olives, walnuts, almonds, tomatoes, quince, apricots, plums; home-raised rabbits, chicken, and pork. Homemade jams and herbal teas.

Climate: Generally warmer than Luján de Cuyo and the Uco Valley. Nights are cool.

Old Trees and High Pergolas

Today, urban sprawl has taken over much of the agricultural land near Mendoza City. But farther east, small towns and villages abound in a vibrant rural community that bikes to work and enjoys a life similar to that lived by their parents and grandparents. As you travel east on the Acceso Este, Ruta 7, the scenery becomes more and more rural, and the trees—eucalyptus, poplar, pepper, olive, and quince—get bigger and bigger. Because of the lower altitude (the vineyards are at between 2400 and 2700 feet [730 and 800 m] in elevation), the climate is warmer and the grapes tend to be less concentrated than those at cooler climates. Some varietals really shine in the east, however, and include Bonarda (Mendoza's second most widely planted red after Malbec), Petit Verdot, and Tempranillo (of Spanish origin). If grown in the *parral*, or traditional pergola system, these varietals can have extraordinary quality in the east. The *parral* pergola creates a sort of umbrella that shields the grapes from the intense sun, generates a cooler microclimate within the canopy, and protects them from frost because of its height (see "El Parral: The High-Pergola Trellis System of the East," page 73).

In the 1980s, my father's research on temperature and quality led him to plant in cooler areas such as Gualtallary (at almost five thousand feet [1500 m], the highest area in Tupungato) and in the southern sections of the Uco Valley. Although we had many emotional ties to the east—this was where my great-grandfather Nicola first settled—my father realized early on that Chardonnay, Malbec, and Cabernet Sauvignon would perform best in the cooler climates of the Uco Valley.

We still owned a fair amount of land in the east, though, and year after year we experimented with water stress and yield reduction to assess its impact on quality. One of our best vineyards in the east is an old Bonarda vineyard that surrounds the family's hundred-year-old summer house, La Vendimia, in El Mirador. In 1997, after a bout of early hail, we harvested a part of the La Vendimia Bonarda with very low yields. We were struck by the quality of the juice, the incredibly intense aromas, and lengthy mouthfeel. Bonarda is a late-ripening variety, and remarkably, even in this warm area, it doesn't ripen until mid-April.

We have also found that Petit Verdot and Syrah yield very aromatic and drinkable wines in the east. Petit Verdot in Bordeaux is known for its somewhat harsh tannins, but in eastern Mendoza, if ripened correctly, it makes a really delicious wine, with the typical red fruit aromatics of Petit Verdot and a smoothness that is rare for the varietal.

Wineries in the area include Familia Zuccardi (see page 74); Argento, an English-Argentine partnership; and Bodegas Esmeralda (home of our family's Tilia brand).

The Mighty Hail

Hail is a natural phenomenon that affects many viticultural areas in the world. Generally speaking, in Mendoza, there is a one in ten chance every year that a vineyard will be hit by hail. Some areas—like the hail "Bermuda triangle" of El Carrizal in Luján de Cuyo—have more hail than others. El Carrizal has very few vineyards. For a grower with only one vineyard, hail-netting is essential, unless one is not prone to heartbreak. My friends David Smith and Sonia Ruseler planted a gorgeous property in Altamira, Finca Alegria ("Happiness Vineyard"). In 2006, half of their vineyard was decimated by hail. They cried their hearts out and then proceeded to hail-net the entire vineyard. Others lack the resources to do this; hail-netting is very expensive.

Some people take the "It's God's will" approach to hail and simply pray for it not to happen. Others purchase cannons that shoot into the sky or hire planes to break up the gray hail clouds. My grandfather Domingo Vicente Catena had anti-hail cannons placed throughout his vineyards and hired *benandanti*, witch doctors, to cast a "luck- generating" spell on each vine. My father, a Ph.D. in economics, tried to persuade him to stop investing in methodologies that had never been proven to work. But my grandfather was not the kind to take adversity lying down; he preferred to do something useless rather than do nothing.

Hail forms when cumulus clouds rise up from the warm earth into a cool sky above. When the humidity hits the cold air, it causes clouds to release ice balls of different sizes—ice balls that can damage a vineyard beyond recognition. It might be summer, but in the wake of a hailstorm, the vines will be stripped of leaves and grapes and the ground will be littered with white ice rocks that look like snowfall.

The reason Mendoza gets more hail than other areas is that the air is so dry that a humid cloud can easily turn into hail when it hits a cold dry front. It is this same continental mountain climate that gives us cool nights and wide night/day temperature differentials, the secret to long hang-times and well-ripened grapes. I believe this is nature's way of telling us there is no such thing as a free ride.

Hail remains a significant problem in eastern Mendoza, even worse than in the Luján de Cuyo and Uco Valley areas. I remember as a child sitting inside the house around the dinner table, hearing the hail hit the metal roof and watching my grandfather's face turn gloomy. No one would speak or say anything, and when it was over we would all walk outside to witness the destruction. My brother, Ernesto, and I would follow my father and grandfather from afar as they began to calculate the financial loss. Although it was tempting to pick up the huge ice rocks to play with, we never did. It just didn't seem right.

The Gaucho

Today, the gaucho is a nationally admired figure, the epitome of the proud Argentine, a man who rides horses bareback, can lasso an escaping steer, and brings justice with the knife. His dress, his manliness, his ruggedness is admired by all Argentines, rich and poor, and even more by foreigners.

In the nineteenth century, however, the gaucho was a controversial figure. Before land rights were given, the open pampas belonged to no one. The mixed-blood gauchos, whose ancestors included Native Amerindians, had long lived a nomadic lifestyle on these lowland plains, where they raised and sold cattle. Once the land was distributed to wealthy families and military men by the Spaniards and, after independence, by the Argentine government, the gauchos were stripped of land they considered rightfully theirs, and they became synonymous with banditry and theft. The landed aristocracy attempted to subdue the gauchos into working for them in an orderly manner. Some gave in; others didn't. Many gauchos refused to give up their nomadic lifestyle and died either in jail or by gunfire. A certain animosity still exists today between hired gauchos and their bosses, and everyone knows that a gaucho must always be treated with respect . . . or else. In 1832, a French chargé d'affaires visiting Argentina wrote that gauchos "are always mounted, they never quit the back of a horse . . . [they are] constantly engaged in ham-stringing and slaughtering cattle, they have engrafted the ferocity of the butcher on the simple habits of the shepherd and are both ignorant and cruel." Only a year later, Charles Darwin recorded a more favorable impression: "The gauchos or country people are very superior to those who reside in towns. The gaucho is invariably most obliging, polite and hospitable. I have not met one instance of rudeness or inhospitality." (Darwin also remarked on the gauchos' penchant for knife fighting, which frequently resulted in bloodshed.) Gauchos were known for spending their free time in *pulperias*, the grocery stores/bars where most of the social life in small villages occurred.

These days, many men who care for cattle and horses throughout Argentina call themselves gauchos. If you drive around the countryside, you are certain to run into boys and men of all ages dressed in the traditional gaucho attire of wide pants that narrow at the ankles (*bombachas*), colorful belts, and French-style berets (*boinas*), with a knife inserted in a sheath that is tucked into the pants' waist in the back. Some wear this attire on special occasions, much as a Texan cowboy would wear chaps and a ten-gallon hat to a rodeo. Many men, like my brother, who is an avid horseman, wear gaucho attire during the weekends, especially if they are riding. Boys in families where there is a gaucho tradition look forward to the day when they can wear their first gaucho uniform.

Gauchito Gil: The Red Gaucho of the Provinces

If you drive around Mendoza, you'll see by the side of the road shrines covered in red cloth and featuring a small gaucho dressed in red. These are shrines to Gauchito Gil. Gil was a gaucho who deserted the army in the province of Corrientes and then became a sort of Argentine Robin Hood, stealing from the rich to give to the poor while wearing a red gaucho outfit. Throughout Mendoza Province, you will see Gauchito Gil shrines filled with red flags and artifacts.

The biggest and most impressive shrine in Mendoza is on the Ruta 40 that leads from Luján de Cuyo to San Carlos. Legend has it that when a policeman caught Gauchito Gil and was about to kill him, Gil told the policeman that his son was ill and that he—Gil—could save him. The policeman killed Gauchito Gil anyway, and the next day found out that his son was sick. He then proceeded to give Gil a proper burial; supposedly thanks to that, his son recovered. In Mendoza, Gauchito Gil shrines are thought to protect drivers from accidents, and those who make an offering hope to experience the expansive healing properties of Gauchito Gil.

El Parral: The High-Pergola Trellis System of the East

There is nothing more romantic than having a picnic under a *parral* (pergola) in Mendoza. If it's lunchtime, stepping under a *parral* provides relief from the bright sun. The east is a warmer, lower-altitude area than Luján de Cuyo or the Uco Valley, and that's why the high-trellised *parral*—where a canopy of leaves covers the grapes and protects them from the intense sun—works so well here. The *parral* is an approximately six-foot-tall (two-meter-tall) pergola with grapes hanging down from the leafy ceiling. *Parrals* (see below) were first developed in Europe and are still in use in areas like the Veneto in Italy and Rias

Baixas in Spain. The *parral* keeps the grapes high above the soil, which protects them from vineyard pests, soil humidity, and frost.

The *parral* was established in Argentina by Italian immigrants. It is called the Venetian *parral*, or *parral* Pini, after winemaker Egisto Pini, who brought the vine-training system to Mendoza in the early twentieth century. Although considered a high-yield training system, if managed well, a *parral* of a certain age can yield extraordinary quality. Good examples of high-quality *parral* vineyards are the one-hundred-year-old *parrals* of Bonarda in Rivadavia and Laborde's old Syrah *parral* in the Uco Valley.

José Alberto Zuccardi

Along the Ruta 7 that heads to eastern Mendoza, you will see signs leading to the Familia Zuccardi winery. The winery was founded in 1963 by José Alberto Zuccardi's father. Fiery and passionate, José Alberto Zuccardi has long championed El Este (the east) as one of the best places to make wine in Mendoza. The Zuccardi family winery was one of the first wineries to dedicate great resources to exporting Argentine wine. In the early days, Zuccardi traveled the globe several times a year selling his wines. I remember sitting in the Bordeaux airport waiting to board a plane at 6:30 A.M., trying to doze off after a week of meetings and late-night dinners at the Vinexpo wine show. Across the aisle sat José Alberto with his computer, phone, and papers sprawled over four seats. He talked, typed, and conducted business until the final boarding call.

What is most interesting at Zuccardi are the fabulous lunches freshly prepared with ingredients grown on the premises, and the experimental vineyard, where the winemakers have planted more than thirty-five varieties—including obscure ones like Caladoc, Bourboulenc, Ancellota, and Ekigaina—to study their adaptation to the conditions in Mendoza. Zuccardi makes wines at many price points. His Q Tempranillo is a classic, a wine where rich fruit is laced with generous oak and has a smoothness and richness in the palate that is truly memorable.

Bonarda: Argentina's Second Most Widely Planted Red Varietal

Up until 2008, if you asked any Argentine winemaker about the origins of Bonarda, he or she would answer that nobody knows the outside-Argentina equivalent of this grape—it's either the same as Bonarda from the Piemonte in Italy, or it is Corbeau (also called Charbonneau in France, or Charbono in the United States). The question was finally answered in 2008 by a group of French and Argentine researchers, who published a paper in the *Journal of Enology and*

José Alberto Zuccardi

Viticulture: Bonarda is none other than the rare Corbeau or Charbonneau of Savoie, a French *département* adjacent to the Italian Alps. There has also been speculation that Charbonneau is the same as Italian Dolcetto, but genetic analysis has shown this to be untrue. The reason for much of the confusion? Both Dolcetto and Charbonneau have large clusters and are called *dulce nero* or *douce noir*—"sweet black"—in their respective countries. But the Argentine Bonarda makes a much richer wine that ripens late in the season, as opposed to the earlier-ripening, lighter-tasting Dolcetto. Both varietals share a fruitiness and intensity of the nose.

There are more than 62,500 acres (25,000 hectares) of Malbec in Argentina and about 50,000 acres (20,000 hectares) of Bonarda, making it Argentina's second most widely planted red. Yet it is harder to find good-quality Bonarda than Malbec. The best sources are old vineyards in the east in places such as Rivadavia, where yields are kept low and water is restricted. For a large part of its history in Argentina, Bonarda was used as a blending grape or even drained of its color to make pink wines like white Zinfandel. Today, several producers, such as Altos las Hormigas, Mayol, Nieto Senetiner, Zuccardi, Tilia, and Tikal, are making serious wines with Bonarda. A good Bonarda has very fruity aromatics—almost like Pinot Noir—and a silky texture that is lighter than Malbec's. The jury is still out as to whether an age-worthy Bonarda can be made.

MAIPÚ AND NORTHERN LUJÁN DE CUYO
At a Glance

Getting There: This area is located 5 to 20 miles (8 to 30 km) south of Mendoza City, between the city and the Mendoza River. To get to Maipú, drive south on the Ruta 40 and exit east on the Carril Rodríguez Peña. For northern Luján de Cuyo, you can either continue on the Ruta 40 south and exit at various locations, or take the Ruta Panamericana south, where you exit a bit closer to the wineries in Mayor Drummond, Chacras de Coria, and Vistalba.

Where to Go: La Rural Wine Museum, wineries, and the quaint colonial town of Chacras de Coria, which has many restaurants and a Sunday *feria* (carnival) and flea market in the central square.

Wines/Varietals: Old-vine Malbec and Cabernet Sauvignon.

Food: This area has become more urbanized in the last decade, and many orchards and vineyards have been replaced by homes. Sample both fancy and simple versions of Argentine and local Mendozan cuisines at La Bourgogne restaurant (fancy) and at numerous restaurants in Chacras de Coria. For some of the best artisanal fruit and vegetable preserves and a fabulous tasting menu (including rose petal confiture and grilled eggplant with garlic), head to Almacén del Sur on your way out of the La Rural Wine Museum.

Climate: Cooler than in Mendoza City, with a pleasant afternoon breeze.

The First Zone

Primera Zona, which stretches all the way down from western Maipú to southern Luján de Cuyo, is the area where European immigrants first established their wineries in the late nineteenth and early twentieth centuries. Some of the oldest names in Argentine wine have their wineries in the Maipú and northern Luján de Cuyo areas: La Rural (Rutini family); Luigi Bosca (Arizu family); Lagarde (today owned by the Pescarmona family); Nieto Senetiner (owned by Perez Companc, one of the richest families in Argentina); Benegas; Trapiche; Pascual Toso; Bodegas Lopez; and Bodega Vistalba, a relatively new facility owned by the well-known Carlos Pulenta of the very influential Pulenta wine family. The area also has several foreign-owned wineries, including Fabre Montmayou (Herve Joyaux Fabre being the first in the recent wave of French investors to Argentina); Altos las Hormigas, owned by three celebrated Italian winemakers; Alta Vista, an old, beautifully refurbished winery owned by the D'Aulans French Champagne family; Trivento, owned by Chile's Concha y Toro; and Enrique Foster, owned and founded by the Spanish-American winemaker Enrique Foster. (For more Primera Zona, Luján de Cuyo wineries, see Chapters 6 and 7.)

Many in Mendoza—locals and foreign investors alike—believe that the freedom to source grapes from different areas is a great advantage in our region. When components from different *terroirs* and altitudes are blended, the resulting wines develop layers of aromas and flavors. I discovered the miracle of what I call "Mendoza microclimate blending" when I started making the blends for my wine Luca in 1999.

Today, many of the wineries in the Primera Zona source their grapes both locally and in the Uco Valley. Because there is no well-established system of appellations in Mendoza, any winery can make a wine from grapes sourced in the various viticultural districts. The only government requirement is that 100 percent of the grapes come from the district or region stated on the label (in the United States, only 85 percent of the grapes have to come from the location on the label; in Europe, it's generally 100 percent). Therefore, a winery like Mendel has its winery located in Mayor Drummond, Luján de Cuyo, but also owns a vineyard in La Consulta, Uco Valley, more than eighty miles (120 km) away. The label states the different districts of origin—Luján de Cuyo or La Consulta—even if all the wines are vinified in the Luján de Cuyo facility. What is and will continue to be of utmost importance in Mendoza is the quality and *terroir* of the vineyards that a winery owns or has long-term contracts with.

Maipú is closest to Mendoza City, and because of that it is losing much of its vineyard land to urbanization. Fortunately, most of the construction involves low-rise Mission-style and brick houses lined by abundant old trees, so the area still has a countryside feel. For a taste of what Maipú was like in the nineteenth century, visit the La Rural winery and wine museum, an eclectic collection of artifacts from that time period (see "La Rural Wine Museum," below).

Mayor Drummond and Chacras de Coria are located about twenty minutes south of downtown Mendoza City. These suburbs were developed in the early twentieth century as an area of summer homes for Mendoza's aristocracy. Chacras is filled with beautiful old houses, gigantic trees, flower-filled gardens, and casual restaurants, and has a pretty colonial central square. Today it is home to most of the upper and middle management and winemaking personnel at Mendoza's wineries. Immediately south of Chacras, Vistalba is a bit more rural. If you are staying here, you will definitely need a car to get around. Most of Mendoza's bed-and-breakfasts are located in Chacras, with shops and restaurants within walking distance.

La Rural Wine Museum

Rodolfo Reina Rutini spent four decades collecting the wine artifacts displayed in this museum in Maipú. It's a great place to get a full view of the last 150 years of winemaking history in Mendoza. You can see the carriages that transported wine-filled casks to Buenos Aires before the advent of the railroads, as well as the old wooden presses used to make wine in the 1900s. The collection of some forty-five hundred winemaking artifacts is displayed in an old colonial barn. This is Mendoza's most-visited winery, so you are likely to find many Argentines starting their wine country tour at La Rural. The winery has a newer state-of-the-art facility in Tupungato, Uco Valley, called Rutini for the founding family.

Alberto Antonini

Alberto Antonini and I have two important things in common: our favorite wine—Massetto by Tenuta dell'Ornellaia—and a love of *ojo de bife* (rib-eye steak) with chimichurri sauce. Alberto is one of the wine world's most sought-after consultants, with jobs in South Africa, Spain, Romania, Armenia, California, Italy—and Mendoza, of course, since the mid-nineties. Alberto started his wine career working at the family's estate in Tuscany, Poggiotondo. After studying at the most prestigious universities in Italy, Bordeaux, and

California, he made his name as head winemaker for Antinori in Italy. Today, he is a partner at Altos Las Hormigas in Luján de Cuyo and a consulting winemaker for ten Mendoza properties, among them Bodegas Renacer, Melipal, and Nieto Senetiner.

Alberto first visited Mendoza with friends in 1995, and he was immediately impressed. "We found something special here," he says, "the dry climate, the soft, well-drained alluvial soils; the fresh water from the Andes; and—last but not least—still a lot of high-density old-vine Malbec!" Even though Malbec wasn't as drinkable then as it is today—Argentine winemaking has improved

Alberto Antonini

tremendously since that time—Alberto saw the region's potential. "Mendoza's soul is wine," he says. "It's not just a business—it goes beyond that. We felt like we were in one of the old established European wine regions."

Now, more than a decade later, Alberto has definite ideas on the future of Argentine wine. "I feel we are moving toward developing in a stronger way the concept of origin and *terroir*, trying slowly to get rid of the varietal concept that is undoubtedly the shortcut to the consumer but in the long term is too generic and weak a concept." For Alberto, it is the wine culture of Mendoza that should be cherished and preserved. "It's essential to make wines that talk of the land, that have a sense of place and are more related to the people and their stories," he says. "In a global world we don't have to be a commodity but a region where you can experience a lot more."

Alberto's philosophy is to find the perfect balance between tradition and innovation, to make wines that are, in his own words, "elegant, with a sense of place."

Roberto de la Mota

Roberto de la Mota: When the Son Is as Good as the Father

Roberto de la Mota has an encyclopedic knowledge of Argentine viticultural history, Malbec, and basically anything to do with Argentine wine. His father, Raúl de la Mota, was the famous winemaker behind the Weinert Estrella, a Cabernet Sauvignon–Malbec blend that was one of the first wines from Argentina to get the attention of Robert Parker, Jr., of *The Wine Advocate* journal. Roberto grew up in Godoy Cruz at the old Arizu winery, where his father was winemaker. Émile Peynaud, the famous winemaker who revolutionized French wine after World War II and who made it his life's work to eradicate off odors and brettanomyces (a kind of yeast that gives barnyard aromas to wine) from the wines in his native France, was a close friend of Roberto's father. When Roberto was a teenager, Peynaud told him that he should study viticulture and not enology, because without understanding the vineyard he would never make a great wine.

And so it is that Roberto studied agronomy first in Mendoza and then headed for a master's degree in viticulture and winemaking at the Université de Montpellier. He started his winemaking career at Weinert and then became head winemaker at Terrazas (the Chandon still-wine property), where he was the first winemaker for the Cheval des Andes Cabernet Sauvignon–Malbec, a wine made in association with Château Cheval Blanc in Bordeaux. Today, Roberto is co-owner of Mendel Winery in Luján de Cuyo with Annabelle Sielecki and consults for several wineries, including NQN in Neuquén.

Roberto understands Mendozan viticulture and winemaking as do few others in our region. As a second-generation winemaker, he has a special sense of the history of Argentina and a pride in the great steps we have taken to elevate the quality of our wines. Despite a terrible accident two years ago that left him wheelchair-bound, Roberto continues to drive all over Mendoza, and is making some of Argentina's most profound wines.

Chapter VI:
LUJÁN DE CUYO:
PERDRIEL

LUJÁN DE CUYO: PERDRIEL
At a Glance

Getting There: Drive about 25 minutes south of Mendoza City on Ruta 40 and exit at Calle Urquiza.

Where to Go: The Terrazas, Norton, Viña Cobos, Achaval-Ferrer, Ruca Malen, Bodegas Renacer, and Melipal wineries.

Wines/Varietals: Cabernet Sauvignon and Malbec.

Food: Argentine *asado*, free-range chicken, olives, tomatoes, onions, garlic.

Climate: A bit warmer than in the Uco Valley. The weather is ideal for making Cabernet Sauvignon and a jammy, ripe style of Malbec.

A Who's Who of Winemaking in Perdriel

Perdriel marks the beginning of the winery corridor of Mendoza, which starts after the Ruta 40 (Highway 40) crosses the Mendoza River and includes, from north to south, the districts of Perdriel, Agrelo, and Ugarteche, all located in Luján de Cuyo. The Ruta 40 is the main highway that crosses through Argentina, from the northern city of La Quiaca in Jujuy Province to the Straits of Magellan in the southern tip of Patagonia. If you are ever in the mood for an adventure, consider driving the entire Ruta 40 as it crosses Argentina. It is a thrilling journey that gives the traveler a true sense of the magnitude of wide-open land in Argentina and its incredible diversity in climate and geography.

In Luján de Cuyo, Mendoza, the Ruta 40 is lined with a who's who of winemaking. You may want to check into the Cavas Wine Lodge, leave your car behind, and mosey around on a bicycle so that you can drink with ease and work off the winery lunches. Even on a warm summer day, you will be cool while riding under the gigantic poplar trees that line each dirt road in the area. There are no sidewalks, so you may find yourself sharing the street with children walking to school, buses, harvest trucks, stray cats and dogs, and families walking or biking to work. Old adobe houses with cracked walls, pretty wildflower gardens, and clothes hanging on outdoor lines share the landscape with beautifully restored wineries. The area has several important wineries, some new, some old. The oldest, Norton, is unique in that its vineyards completely surround the winery. Terrazas is the still-wine facility of the world-renowned Moët et Chandon, which has facilities in France and California. It makes a whole range of wines at different prices under the Terrazas label and has a prestigious joint venture with Bordeaux's Cheval Blanc winemaker, Pierre Lurton, named Cheval des Andes.

Cobos is Paul Hobbs's winery with his Argentine partners Luis Barraud and Andrea Marchiori. Bodegas Renacer—where famed Tuscan winemaker Alberto Antonini is consultant—is making fabulous Malbecs under the Punto Final label. Achaval-Ferrer is a decade-old partnership between Santiago Achaval and the renowned Tuscan wine consultant Roberto Cipresso. Achaval-Ferrer has shaken up the area by releasing high-priced single-vineyard wines that have garnered accolades from the press (see the Bella Vista Vineyard profile, page 94). Other wineries in the area include Melipal and Ruca Malen, where Lucas Bustos, the chef who made his name cooking for wineries in Luján de Cuyo, prepares delicious meals drawn from recipes that he spent years obtaining, in his own words, from "little old country ladies" who were locally famous for their cooking.

Paul Hobbs: Unstoppable Winemaker

I first met Paul Hobbs in 1989 when he had just started consulting for my father in Argentina. He had a lofty pedigree in winemaking, coming off stints at Opus One, Mouton Rothschild, and Simi after graduating with a master's degree in viticulture from UC Davis. Paul's good looks and warm, easy-going personality can be deceiving. He is one of the most intense perfectionists I have ever met. When Paul arrived at our winery, Bodegas Esmeralda, he put signs on every wall saying *"Atención a los detalles"*: "Pay Attention to the Details." Paul worked with my father for eight years and was incredibly influential in redefining the way we

Paul Hobbs

made wine, adhering to the highest standards of classical French winemaking. To this day, Paul, my father, and our family's winemaker of twenty-five years, José Galante, share a very special mutual admiration and friendship.

Paul consults for over a dozen wineries in Argentina, including Gascón, Rutini, Toso, and Finca Decero, and has devoted himself to promoting and improving the quality of Argentine wine. Paul's winery, Cobos, which he owns in partnership with Luis Barraud and Andrea Marchiori, has established itself as one of Argentina's leading Malbec producers. And in California, Hobbs's namesake winery in Sebastopol is making some of the country's most sought-after wines.

So what is Paul Hobbs' secret, and why do his wines get such high ratings from the critics? Answers Paul: "Select an outstanding *terroir*, work with it until you know it well, pay attention to the details, and don't over-manipulate the grapes; just let Mother Nature do the work. The resulting wines will be elegant and true to their *terroir*." Paul described how he felt seeing Mendoza for the first time: "It was 1989. I did not have high expectations. The wines I had tasted were oxidized, but then when I entered the country from Chile, driving across the Andes, I saw the small vines with small clusters that reminded me of France, and I knew that great wines could be possible. It was exciting when I met Nicolás Catena, who wanted to change everything about how wines were being made in Argentina. He wanted to make the best wines in the world and would stop at nothing. Today, I can confidently say that Argentina is making some of the best and most profound wines on the planet."

Michael Halsrick:
Scion and Adventurer Turned Argentine Ambassador

We call him El Aleman (the German), but the truth is that after living in Mendoza for over two decades, Michael, a.k.a. Miguel, is just as Argentine as the rest of us. Miguel belongs to the family that owns the Swarovski empire, and he is the brains behind Norton, the family winery that he has resuscitated and turned into one of Argentina's leading exporters.

Miguel has a genuine love for his adopted land. "When I was seventeen," he told me, "my father, Gernot Langes, said to me you can either go to college or learn what a dollar is worth." Miguel picked the latter and proceeded to work as a deposit stockboy and door-to-door salesperson in Venezuela, as a mechanic at Fiat Buenos Aires, and as a gaucho in Chaco and Salta—where he decided that he didn't like riding horses or getting up at three in the morning, but that he did have a talent for sales. Years later, after finishing college and obtaining a business degree in the United States, he was working at a bank in Austria when his father offered him the job of running Bodega Norton, the winery that his family had acquired in 1989 in the middle of one of Argentina's many financial crises.

Norton is one of Argentina's oldest wineries, founded by the Englishman Edward Norton, who came to Argentina to build the railroads in the 1860s. Miguel has made a great deal of quality improvements to his Perdriel vineyards and winemaking facilities and has created an Argentine classic that is sold around the world. When I asked him what he thinks about Argentina, he answered: "It was and is the last jewel to be found in the world of wine."

When I asked him how he has managed to survive in a country that is so unstable politically and economically, "What doesn't kill you makes you stronger," he said. "To be successful in Argentina you need to have a very open mind. You need to know how to lose sometimes, and by losing you figure out how to win. What I love the most about Argentina is the people. Argentines are really good people, they are loyal, and they have a very special pride in the work they do. In every crisis there is an opportunity, and one needs to know how to take advantage of it. We need to focus on quality wines."

Michael Halsrick and his daughter

La Melezca: A Worker's Pittance Spun into Malbec Gold

La melezca is the name given to the few bunches of grapes that are left on the vine after harvest. The grapes may have been missed in a rushed harvest or weren't ripe or large enough to pick—grapes growing on a weak branch, for example, may be smaller and less ripe than the rest of the grapes. Vineyard owners would often donate these bunches to workers so that they could make their own home wine with them. The official harvest was always done as early as possible, because the vineyard owners wanted to get paid and didn't want to risk bad weather ruining the crop. But it turned out that the grapes left on the vine an additional month after the official harvest benefitted from an extra infusion of plant "calories." Today, many winemakers believe that leaving grapes on the vine—especially in a low-production vineyard—can enhance flavors and concentration.

Here is the story of José, a vineyard worker from Luján de Cuyo, who gave a taste of some of his homemade Malbec wine—derived from *melezca* grapes—to High Note winemaker Fernando Buscema. Seventy years old, José has been working in Agrelo since he was a child:

> You know, *mijito*—my child—the best wine is the one made with the *melezca* that comes from the French grape [Malbec]. I have been working this vineyard since I was a child, and the boss always gave me the leftover grapes so that I could make wine to drink at home throughout the year. Generally, the harvest would end in the middle of March, when the grapes had achieved ripeness, because at that time, that is all that the wineries cared about. The price of grapes was not good, so the boss always asked us to be generous in the pruning, in the water and in the compost . . . there should always be plenty of these things. The yields were high; the higher, the better. But as the years went on, everything started to change, and people began to talk about quality. The winemakers started to visit the vineyards and taste the grapes. It was during one of those visits that I shared with the winemaker of a very famous winery one of the wines that I had kept for a long time—more than fifteen years, I think. You should have seen his face! I realized that he accepted the wine just so that he wouldn't offend me. "Taste it," I said to him, "and then you can tell me what you think."
>
> A few days went by, even a few weeks, and the young winemaker came back to see me. "Where did you get that wine?" he asked. Homemade, I answered. The young man was surprised by the color

and the concentration of the wine. He wanted to know exactly how I had been making my home wine for over fifty years. I explained that the grapes had to be "French"—what they call Malbec these days—and that I would harvest the *melezca*, the few bunches left on the vineyard, about thirty days after the harvest was over, when the grapes were really sweet. Then we would separate the berries by hand, all of us, women and children too, and we would step on them so that the juice would begin to boil. "To ferment," said the young winemaker. Every day we would push the "hat" down with an oak stick, three or four times, and then we would take out the clean juice, put it into some big wooden bins that a friend had made for me, and leave it there for a year. By the next January, just before the new harvest started, we put the wine in one-liter bottles and drank it throughout the year.

At the time of this story, Fernando was a recent graduate doing research at the University of Enology in Mendoza. "I learned an important lesson," Fernando told me. "Sometimes there is as much to be learned by talking to the old people as there is by doing research in the laboratory."

Achaval-Ferrer's Bella Vista Vineyard

Santiago Achaval is a relative newcomer to the world of wine, but he is as astute as a fox and has been able to catch up through sheer intelligence and determination. His business savvy comes from a life in real estate in the neighboring Cordoba Province and two years spent at Stanford Business School. But his love for wine, in his own words, is an acquired "bug: contagious, incurable, and terribly damaging to the checking account!" Achaval and his partner, Ferrer, were smart to team up with Roberto Cipresso, an equally passionate individual who understands viticulture to the finest detail from years working as a winemaker all over Italy. What makes the Bella Vista Vineyard in the Perdriel district of Luján de Cuyo particularly beautiful are its old vines, its high-density planting—2,636 plants per acre (6,500/hectare)—the olive trees interspersed among the vines, and the spectacular views of the valley from the edge of the Mendoza River—hence the name Bella Vista ("Beautiful View"). Achaval-Ferrer has done much to promote the distinctive *terroirs* of Argentine Malbec.

AGRELO AND UGARTECHE
At a Glance

Getting There: Head south of Mendoza City on the Ruta 40, pass the Mendoza River and Perdriel, and exit at the Ruta 7 toward Chile. Calle Cobos and Calle Cochabamba, where most of the wineries are located, are near the Ruta 7, within a ½ mile to 2 miles (1 to 1.5 km) from the highway on parallel streets.

Where to Go: Wineries: Bodega Catena Zapata, Dominio del Plata, Belasco de Baquedano, Pulenta Estate, Doña Paula, Dolium, Finca La Anita, Tapiz, Septima.

Wines/Varietals: Old-vine Malbec and Cabernet Sauvignon.

Food: Tomatoes, garlic, onions; fruit orchards; viticultural production dominates because of the historical prestige of wineries and vineyards in the area.

Climate: A bit warmer than in the Uco Valley; the temperatures are similar to those of the Napa Valley in California.

The Napa of Argentina

Perdriel (see Chapter 6) and Agrelo are where many of the better-known export-driven Argentine wineries are located. Three long dirt roads, the Ruta 15, Cochabamba Street, and Cobos Street, lead south from Perdriel to Agrelo and Ugarteche and run parallel to the Ruta 40. All the area wineries are located along these roads. The roads are pitted with potholes, wild dogs and cats run free, and you'll see more than a few horses tied to a tree by the road with no owner in sight. Unhelmeted bikers of all ages ride these roads—so drive slowly. Sparsely populated Agrelo and Ugarteche have a simple country charm, with mostly dirt roads and scattered white adobe and brick houses. You won't find shopping malls here—only some of the biggest names in Argentine wine.

Our family winery, Bodega Catena Zapata, is located on Calle Cobos in Agrelo. The old Cabernet Sauvignon lot at our La Pirámide vineyard, planted in 1982 with a special Mendozan plant selection, has a specific chocolate–black fruit aroma that I can recognize in any blind tasting. The clay soils make it a bit more challenging to farm here, because when it rains, drainage is not optimal, but there is a firmness and tannic structure to the wines of Agrelo and Ugarteche that distinguish them from those of any other valley in Mendoza. The climate is slightly warmer than in the Uco Valley, and the aromas are less flashy, but the wines produced here have an incredible thickness in the mid-palate and an overall elegance that must have something to do with the clay in the soils. Many of the wineries in the area have only been built in the last decade, yet they have managed to make a name by focusing on the top end.

Dominio del Plata, which came out of a partnership between Susana Balbo and Pedro Marchevski, has managed to become one of the leading exporters of fine wine from Argentina in a very short time. Pedro Marchevski started his career working for my grandfather Domingo and was my father's right-hand man for many years. He was the first to teach me about our vineyards, and to this date is a walking encyclopedia about Mendozan wine and viticulture. Pedro possesses a singular combination of work ethic and off-the-charts intelligence. Susana worked with me at Catena Zapata in the export department for several years and always impressed me with her savoir-faire and determination. Susana and Pedro have parted ways (Susana is currently owner and head winemaker), and Pedro has moved on to consult for several wineries and vineyards around Mendoza, including his own family's vineyards. But Dominio remains as strong as ever, making distinctive Argentine wines that are exported all over the world.

Other wineries in the area include Tapiz, which houses a fabulous bed-and-breakfast and restaurant in a colonial-style mansion in nearby Maipú; Dolium; Belasco de Baquedano; the Chilean Doña Paula; the Spanish Séptima, owned by Codorniu; and Pulenta Estate, owned by Eduardo Pulenta and his father, Don Antonio Pulenta, at ninety years old one of the few living witnesses to the beginnings of modern Argentine winemaking.

The Family Jewels

The vista from the Catena Zapata pyramid looks out at the Malbec plant selection that was an important part of our effort to elevate Malbec to the next level in Mendoza. In the early 1990s, under the watchful eye of our vineyard manager, Alejandro Sejanovich, we planted 145 different cuttings of Malbec from our seventy-year-old Angélica vineyard and selected the best—those with the smallest berries and bunches, the lowest yields, the most concentrated aromas and flavors—to plant throughout our vineyards in Mendoza. This plant selection is the equivalent of a family heirloom. Alejandro Sejanovich calls the Catena cuttings "the family jewels," and he is well aware that he is its guardian: "It is my job to make sure that the population of plants is preserved throughout the next generations."

Alejandro Vigil: Catena Zapata's Chief Winemaker

A "crazy man" by his own account, Alejandro Vigil sleeps four hours a night, owns nine dogs, and keeps a cow at his house to provide fresh milk for the children who attend the local school. With his crazy—as in finger-in-the-electric-socket—shock of curly hair, he gives validity to the concept that true geniuses are not normal people. Vigil started working at Catena Zapata in 2002 as winemaker for our research department. He had been asked to resign from his

Alejandro Vigil

job as head of the soils division (at the tender age of twenty-eight) at the INTA (Argentina's National Agriculture Institute) after he decided to make his own set of wines from the research parcels because he objected to the Institute's winemaking protocols. This man is a born winemaker. Wine is in his blood, he feels wine, he drinks fine wine as if tomorrow were his last day on earth, and he knows instinctively, after tasting grapes from a specific parcel, how long the fermentation and maceration should be, how many rackings will be necessary, and what kind and age of oak will be best suited for the wine's *élevage*. Although he is a chemist by training, most of what he does is by instinct. "Wine was not made to have a recipe," he says. "Recipes are the death of wine. Every parcel needs to be vinified separately; every lot needs to have its own harvest time, winemaking, maceration time, time in barrel." Vigil explains why he is the

Nicolás and Elena Catena

way he is: "You see, I am a mix of many cultures; I am part Arab, part Jew, part Asturian, part Venetian. I grew up with wine." At Vigil's grandfather's house, every grandchild had a job. The grapes were pressed by hand in a colander, and it was four-year-old Alejandro's job to harvest the fruit, wash it, and take out the seeds. Then his grandfather would put the juice through a woman's nylon stocking and pour the day's labor into a plastic bin. "My grandfather would drink a few glasses before his nap and give me a glass of it mixed with soda," says Vigil. "It was a great honor to receive this drink from my grandfather; he only gave it to the children who worked hard."

I asked Vigil what he considers to be the greatest changes of the last decade in Argentine winemaking. "The first big change," he answers, "was to vinify the Malbec and the Cabernet Sauvignon differently, to stop thinking of these two varietals as one and the same. We are not Bordeaux; we are Mendoza. We now understand each vineyard, each lot, each plant."

The Catena Zapata Pyramid

Our winery is built in the shape of a pyramid. The pyramid faces the majestic Andes, as if paying homage to them, and looks as if it has always been here. My father built the pyramid in the late 1990s when it became clear that the old family winery—Bodegas Esmeralda—was too far from the vineyards of the high-altitude Uco Valley, where much of the best fruit was grown.

My husband, Daniel, took my father and architect Pablo Sánchez Elia on a tour of the Napa Valley to study the architecture of high-end wineries in the New World. My father had entertained the thought of building in the style of his Italian or Spanish forefathers, or in the traditional Mission or Italian Renaissance style, like many other Mendoza wineries. That was before my brother Ernesto and I, who had spent time traveling through Central America, encouraged my father to visit the ruins of Tikal. He had always had an interest in the Mayan culture, so he traveled to Tikal with my mother, Elena. Both felt a spiritual connection to the place. "The Mayans were the most advanced Indian culture of the Americas," he said. "They wished to excel in science, art,

and culture. Our goals were similar. Besides, I wanted our family winery to have an architectural style that emphasized the uniqueness of our high-altitude Andean *terroir*, one that would be completely different from that of Europe and North America." Today, the winery stands in the middle of the La Pirámide vineyard. It is built with locally sourced and cut rocks that create a beautifully rugged surface texture. A central shaft allows sunlight to enter the building, sending beams of pure light all the way to the underground caves.

Own-Rooted Vines: Where Old World Meets New World

Winemakers in France and North America have made their names by using own-rooted, or ungrafted, vines to make their wines. Didier Dagueneau, the iconic Loire producer who died tragically in an airplane crash in 2008, celebrated the über-presence of *terroir* in his Asteroide cuvée of Sauvignon Blanc made out of own-rooted vines. Gary Pisoni, of Monterey County, has become known for planting ungrafted Pinot Noir in California. Everybody has been waiting since the 1980s for the Pisoni vines to become infested by phylloxera—but they haven't. Pisoni's ungrafted grapes are among the most sought-after in the area.

Although most of the world's famous wines are made from grafted vines, proponents of ungrafted vines believe that an own-rooted vine will achieve a better balance with its soil and climate—its *terroir*—than a vine grafted onto the trunk of an American rootstock, the trunk of a vine destined to make table grapes. Also, grafting generates uniformity of growth and vigor in a vineyard, whereas ungrafted plants are less homogenous and provide a variability of flavors that makes the final wine more interesting, say ungrafted vine proponents—like the many instruments in a symphony.

It is extremely risky to plant an ungrafted vineyard in Europe, North America, South Africa, and some parts of Australia because of the prevalence of phylloxera in these regions. In the nineteenth century, just as Malbec was taking off in Argentina, the phylloxera louse was decimating vineyards all over the world. (Argentina was spared for the same reason that it is spared today—because the louse does not survive in the country's dry climate and sandy soils.) Later, in the 1980s, it happened all over again, this time in the Napa Valley, when it was discovered that the rootstocks in use were no longer phylloxera resistant.

A grafted vine is a *Vitis vinifera* plant. Most of the world's good wines are made from *Vitis vinifera* (think Cabernet Sauvignon, Syrah, Merlot, Malbec) grafted onto an American rootstock trunk, which is resistant to the phylloxera

louse. The grapes produced on this grafted vine are of the *Vitis vinifera* variety; only the trunk and roots are of the American rootstock. Vines are also grafted to prevent infestation by nematodes, a kind of parasite that can affect grapevines. In Argentina, more than 90 percent of the vines are ungrafted, or grown on their original rootstocks, and many vineyards are quite old, as they have never suffered destruction by phylloxera, which would have led to early replanting. Although there are areas with small amounts of phylloxera, especially in the Luján de Cuyo region where the soils have a significant clay component, the flying louse that spreads the disease by laying eggs cannot survive in dry air. Phylloxera also does not thrive in the predominantly sandy soils of the Uco Valley.

Own-rooted vines can have less foliage and be less productive than grafted vines. Some winemakers in France believe that the wines there were better and more representative of their *terroir* prior to grafting. Others believe that grafted vines are healthier—and that healthier vines make better wines. Yet the ungrafted vines in Argentina, which have long roots that dig widely into the ground, seem to react better to environmental stress than grafted vines—their expansive roots never stop giving "life juice" to the grapes on their trunk.

In Argentina, most people plant Chardonnay on grafted vines because the grape is susceptible to nematodes. But most Malbec is planted on its own roots. The French think we are crazy not to graft in Argentina, and that some day we will regret not using American rootstocks. But every year, when my old-vine grapes come in for Luca Malbec and I taste the earth and the fruit and the density of these ungrafted vines, I decide we are doing something right. Once again, I cast my lot with most Argentine-born viticulturalists, who believe that phylloxera doesn't stand a chance in this country. Only the future will tell.

Cavas Wine Lodge

Chapter VIII:
THE UCO VALLEY: TUPUNGATO

THE UCO VALLEY: TUPUNGATO
At a Glance

Getting There: The Uco Valley region comprises (from north to south) the districts of Tupungato, Tunuyán, and San Carlos. To reach Tupungato in the northwest, head south from Mendoza City through Luján de Cuyo on Ruta 40; turn west on Ruta 86 for the town of Tupungato, then south again on Ruta 89 for the area's main wineries. It's about a 70-minute drive from Mendoza City.

Where to Go: The town of Tupungato and the wineries on Ruta 89: Salentein, Rutini, Finca Sophenia, Andeluna, and Masi Tupungato.

Wines/Varietals: Malbec, Cabernet Sauvignon, Chardonnay, and Merlot.

Food: Freshly caught river trout; wild goat and rabbit; quince, apples, peaches, and walnuts; potatoes, onions, squash, and pumpkin.

Climate: Cooler temperatures and greater night-day temperature differentials as one climbs in altitude and gets closer to the Andes in the west.

VINO
MAR 2
10 30 P.M
1922
TRAVEL

An Oasis of Green

Driving southwest of Mendoza and Luján de Cuyo takes you closer to the mountains, and the terrain feels more and more remote. The Ruta 86 leads you through the high desert for about thirty minutes. Here you can get a real feeling for the native flora (cacti and brush) and local climate, where agriculture is only possible thanks to the channeled snowmelt of the Andes Mountains. Heading out of the desert into the Tupungato oasis, you'll see green reappear, with orchards, small gardens, and large trees lining every street. This drive gives you a real sense of how vast and underpopulated Argentina is.

Named after an Indian chief who ruled the area hundreds of years ago, the Uco Valley has optimal soils, cool average temperatures, and large night-day thermal amplitude—meaning that it gets very cold here at night and relatively hot during the day, so the difference between the two can be substantial. The Uco Valley's southern location close to the Andes and the resulting high altitude—3,200 to 5,000 feet (975 to 1,524 m)—make for cooler temperatures. All of these factors explain why the valley has seen so many new vineyard plantings and new wineries in the last decade.

Tupungato is located due southwest of Mendoza City and Luján de Cuyo. The valley is named after the dormant volcano of Tupungato, the single pointy snow-capped mountain that can be seen from almost any place in Mendoza on a clear day. (*Tupungato* means "star observatory" in the Huarpe Indian language, and has nothing to do with *gato*, the Spanish word for cat.) Tupungato is well known for its high-quality fruit and vegetable production.

In the early twentieth century, Italian, Spanish, Syrian, and Lebanese immigrants settled the area, establishing an agricultural tradition of orchards and vineyards. Back then it was not practical to produce wine in the area because of the long distances from Mendoza City, and because it was hard to find laborers to work in the wineries. The soils were rocky, hard to prepare for planting, and shallow—making it a difficult place to obtain the high yields that the immigrants were seeking. For a long time, Uco Valley grapes were sold by independent growers to a few "stock" winemaking facilities that would produce wine and sell it in bulk to wineries in Maipú and Luján de Cuyo. In the last fifteen years, however, a series of new state-of-the-art wineries have been built in Tupungato. The district's incredible potential for producing quality wines is making waves both locally and internationally.

Most of the local inhabitants live in the town of Tupungato, which has a population of almost ten thousand and a fabulous fish restaurant called El Ilo.

At El Ilo, you should order one of the freshly caught river fish in whatever sauce the owner recommends (my favorite is the Provençal) and follow it with a dessert of candied spaghetti squash, cheese, and freshly ground pepper—a house specialty invented by the owner's daughter (they rightfully refused to give me the recipe).

Mariano di Paola,
Rutini Tupungato's winemaker

The Wineries of Tupungato

If you take the Ruta 89 due southwest from the town of Tupungato, you will come across the main wineries in the area: Andeluna, the Rutini Tupungato winery, Salentein, and Finca Sophenia. The Dutch-owned Salentein has mounted an impressive complex that includes a gorgeous winery, a world-class art museum (Killka), a chapel, and a posada that serves meals and has a beautiful garden and swimming pool on the premises. Andeluna, set in a gorgeous new Italianate structure, is owned by the American H. Ward Lay, of the Frito-Lay family, who lives half the year in a ranch he owns in Patagonia. I've heard from several tour guides that Andeluna can arrange Argentine cooking lessons on the premises. Rutini is the brand-new Tupungato facility of the La Rural Winery (home to the Wine Museum) in Maipú. It was built by the Bórmida & Yanzón architectural firm (see page 116). The Rutini family was one of the first to plant fine varietals in Tupungato in the 1940s, and the new winery was built near one of the family's old vineyards. Not too far from Rutini Winery is Finca

Sophenia, the property of the well-known former Wines of Argentina president Roberto Luka, who is making highly awarded wines that are well distributed throughout Argentina, North America, and Europe.

Masi Tupungato, a label by the well-known Venetian Amarone producer, sources its grapes from an old vineyard in Los Arboles, Tupungato, and has a small winery nearby. The Masi Passo Doble is a blend of Malbec and dried Corvina grapes from the Veneto, Italy, where the Masi family comes from. They call it wine with "Argentinean soul and Venetian style," and this deep, dark, concentrated wine is a bit tannic when young but develops beautifully in the bottle.

Eliana Bórmida and daughter

Bórmida and Yanzón:
The Architects of Mendoza's New-Winery Revolution

One would hardly imagine that the O. Fournier winery (located farther south in La Consulta) and Salentein were built by the same architects, but they were. Eliana Bórmida and Mario Yanzón are responsible for many of the new wineries built in Mendoza over the last ten years. The husband-and-wife architectural firm of Bórmida & Yanzón is known for generating a new style and a new point of view with every project. *Food & Wine* magazine called the O. Fournier winery "a hypermodern fantasy" that "looks like a space-age beetle." Salentein, on the other hand, resembles something Frank Lloyd Wright might have imagined if his favorite medium had been cement. Both wineries have stunning Andes Mountains backdrops. "With Salentein, we were trying to highlight the relationship between the architecture of the winery and its Andean surroundings to create images with a strong local identity, capable of communicating our Mendoza to the global markets," says Eliana, who has kept her maiden name, Bórmida, and worked her way through four children and thirty major winery projects. Eliana summarizes the firm's philosophy: "We work with very different materials and methods, always earthquake resistant, where the structures play a protagonistic role. We don't believe in styles, but we do believe in expressivity and in character as essential values in architecture." Bórmida & Yanzón have designed new wineries for Salentein, Septima, O. Fournier, Vistalba, Rutini Tupungato, Sophenia, and Dolium, among others, and remodeled traditional wineries including Norton, Flichman, Navarro Correas, Pulenta Estate, and Antigal.

The ABC's of High-Altitude Desert Viniculture

Mendoza is a winemaking region like no other. From each and every location, the west is defined by the snow-capped Andes. As you follow the curve of the Andes from west or south, the mountain views become more and more prominent—you have the feeling that the mountains lie just a stone's throw away. Mendoza's wine country, located in the high plains by the foothills of these majestic peaks, has a privileged *terroir*: very cold nights, intense sunlight, and a signature varietal, Malbec, that is capable of making profound wines.

But Mendoza also has something else: high altitude. Situated in valleys at altitudes between 2,700 and 5,000 feet (823 and 1,524 m) above sea level, the region benefits from a dry continental climate, lots of sunshine, and a pronounced night-day temperature differential. Altitude has two important effects on grape growing: one is a cooling effect on temperature, and another is a dramatic increase in sunlight intensity. Greater heights mean lower temperatures. In Mendoza, the calculation is that for every 328 feet (100 m) of increased altitude, the average temperature decreases 1.8 degrees Fahrenheit (1°C). Greater sunlight means thicker grape skins (the grapevine's attempt to protect its seeds from the sun), which are rich in tannins and polyphenols—the flavor-giving compounds in wine—explaining why Mendoza's high-altitude wines are so rich and flavorful.

My father, Nicolás Catena, pioneered extreme high-altitude viticulture in Mendoza, and was the first to plant a Malbec vineyard at almost 5,000 feet (1,524 m) elevation. He has been called the man who discovered and defined the benefits of high-altitude viticulture in Argentina.

Today, it seems obvious that one of the keys to obtaining better quality and concentration in Mendozan wines is to plant in climates that are closer in average temperatures to the famed regions of Bordeaux and Napa and the even cooler climes of Burgundy. But in the 1980s, when my father began his quest for quality, this was anything but obvious. In fact, most of the vineyards considered the best at the time were in the relatively warm, lower-altitude Maipú area, below 3,000 feet (914 m) elevation.

Studying the soils, climate, and sunlight intensity of high-altitude Mendoza, we found that our *terroir* was so different from that of France and the rest of the world that most of the Old World viticultural rules could not be applied here. In fact, the research that we did at Catena in the 1990s showed that in Mendoza we could perfectly ripen Malbec and Cabernet Sauvignon in places like Gualtallary, Tupungato, with a climate as cold as that of Burgundy (nobody would ever think of planting Cabernet Sauvignon in Burgundy). The lesson we learned was that our region has its own set of rules.

The Low-Fertility Desert Soils of Mendoza

People are often surprised when I tell them that Mendoza is a high desert with less than 8 inches (20 cm) of rainfall a year. Intuitively, deserts and vineyards seem an incongruous match. But our dry alluvial soils are part of the secret behind Mendoza's best wines. The early European immigrants were often frustrated by the low fertility of the Uco Valley and preferred the eastern region with its more fertile clay soils. They watered by flooding the vineyards— the only way to get higher yields.

Today, we are looking for balance and low yields. We prize our low-fertility soils, where the vines have to suffer a little, the plants have low vigor, and the grape clusters are small, exactly the way we want them. In the words of Jacques Lurton, one of the French pioneers of Argentina's wine revolution: "Mendoza has an unquestionable advantage over other Southern Hemisphere countries in the quality of its soils. Millions of years of geologic activity have given these alluvial soils at the foot of the Andes a unique structure, which is extremely well adapted to viticulture. It is because of its *terroir* that I have great personal faith in Mendoza as the region capable of producing the most complex and interesting wines of the Southern Hemisphere."

The soils of Mendoza are filled with rocks and pebbles that were deposited by rivers and glaciers millions of years ago. It is the gravelly, rocky nature of our soil that makes it well drained; good drainage prevents the pooling of water on the ground, which can dilute grapes and cause vine rot and other diseases that come from overly humid soils and air. Because of the dry air and lack of rain, the soils of Mendoza are heterogeneous—clay, sand, and limestone are mixed rather than in layers—and have difficulty holding onto nutrients. The soils in areas where it rains more—most of Europe, North America, and South Africa, for example—develop distinct layers of clay, sand, and limestone and have a higher amount of nutrients than the soils of Mendoza. The rains allow the soil to retain organic matter and force the various soil components to layer according to their weight.

Glorious wines can be made in many different kinds of soils. But after years of studying the soils and climate of Mendoza, I can honestly say that every vineyard parcel in Mendoza has a different combination of sand, clay, lime, and rocks from a parcel only a few feet away, and subtle variations in altitude and latitude can dramatically change the aromas and flavors of an Argentine wine. It is this diversity of vineyard lots, of regions within regions, that makes it possible for our wines to have specific regional and vineyard characteristics that simply cannot be reproduced in any other part of the world.

Although the soils are very different throughout the province, one can make some generalizations. The clay tends to lie at the top above the lime, while sand is mixed in at the bottom. Some areas have deep topsoils (the layer of soil above the *canto rodado*—rocky subsoil), while others have more shallow topsoils. Areas with a shallower, rocky topsoil, such as most of Altamira in the southern Uco Valley, tend to have lower fertility, excellent drainage, and optimal conditions for low-yielding, high-quality Malbec. Areas with deeper topsoils and a higher amount of clay, such as those in eastern Mendoza, tend to be more fertile and produce higher-yielding vines and less-concentrated grapes.

The Sustainable Power of Irrigation

Mendoza is blessed with a true continental climate—meaning that it is shielded from the influence of the ocean. This is unique in the world of wine, where most viticultural regions lie near the ocean. A somewhat similar region would be Washington state, except that Washington state is not as high in altitude as Mendoza. In Mendoza, it usually rains in the summer, often around the time of harvest, but the rains are very brief and generally have little impact on quality. In 1998, when El Niño brought three straight weeks of rain to Mendoza, it had a significant and negative impact on the harvest, but nobody, even the very old people, could remember such a phenomenon ever happening before.

The dry continental climate makes it very easy to farm sustainably in Mendoza. There are a few fungal diseases, such as *peronóspora* and *hoja de malvón*, a vineyard trunk disease—but these are usually treated with sulfur, a natural mineral that is not considered a pesticide.

Today, a great deal of focus is being placed on water conservation around the world. In Mendoza, desert water conservation has been a part of viticulture for many centuries. The head of viticulture at Catena Zapata, Alejandro Sejanovich, who wrote his thesis on water stress at Montpellier University in France in the early nineties, told me, "I wonder if anybody in France understood what I was writing about. In France, where it rains routinely in the winter, irrigation is in the hands of God, not the vintner." Irrigation is forbidden in France (except in a few areas) by laws meant to control vineyard yields. In Mendoza, there would be no viticulture if there were no irrigation. And we only have water for farming thanks to the eternally snow-capped Andes, to the Huarpe Indians who set up the first irrigation canals, and to the water act of 1850, which established that water rights belonged to the land and not to the landowners. Every piece of Mendoza has an assigned amount of water, and this cannot be altered by law. A government official called the *tomero* is the only one who holds the key to the water dam; he opens it at a specific time each week and provides water to each property owner.

Today, most new vineyards are set up to receive water through drip irrigation, the most water-efficient and water-conserving method of irrigation. A great deal of flood irrigation is still going on in some old vineyards and in Eastern Mendoza, where soil salinity benefits because this kind of irrigation removes the salt from the soil.

In Mendoza, conservation is practiced in other ways as well. The water waste from a winery, known as water effluvients, is often used to water the eucalyptus trees that wineries plant just for this purpose. Most wineries provide biodiesel cars for their employees because they are more economical. Many vineyard workers bike or walk to work.

An entire ecosystem of interdependent flora and fauna lives in and around the vineyards, including owls, otters, foxes, hares, gophers, ants, doves, and many kinds of insects. Cover crops are common because they help the soil retain the small amount of fertile nutrients in Mendoza's generally low-fertility soils.

Catena Zapata's Adrianna Vineyard: High Altitude Uncovered

The Adrianna vineyard lies in a beautiful location on the westernmost border of Tupungato, in a small district called Gualtallary, flanked by a small hill that shields it from the winds, and so close to the mountains that one has the sense that the peaks are looking out over the vineyard. Some of our best Malbec is produced here at Adrianna. It's hard to believe that at one time no one in Mendoza thought the varietal could ripen above 4,500 feet (1,370 m) of elevation. But it did—and spectacularly. "Your father was the only one who thought that Malbec would ripen here," says our viticulturalist Alejandro Sejanovich, who was responsible for planting the Adrianna vineyard in the 1990s. At almost 5,000 feet (1,500 m) elevation, two years of temperature calculations had classified the average temperatures before harvest as closest to those in Burgundy, where only early-ripening varieties like Chardonnay and Pinot Noir can mature. But my father had seen how well Chardonnay had ripened in this area, and his theory was that the additional high-altitude sunlight would allow Malbec to ripen even if late in the season. "Besides," he said, "I had to find out what the altitude limit of Malbec cultivation was in Mendoza, and I was willing to make a mistake to get the answer."

The soils here are predominantly sandy, with a bit of lime and round rocks that extend from the surface to the bottom soil. The soils are very poor in organic material and spectacularly drained, so yields are naturally low and berries are small and concentrated, just what you need for a rich and powerful Malbec. It is extraordinary to think that varietals as different as Chardonnay and Malbec can be grown in the same vineyard, but they can in Mendoza. Because of the cool climate (this is the coolest of our family's vineyards), the wines from Adrianna have a minerality in the aromatics and palate that is unusual in wines from other parts of Mendoza. The Malbec, which is selected plant by plant, goes into the Catena Zapata single-vineyard Malbec Adrianna, Malbec Argentino, Catena Alta, and the Bodega Catena Zapata blend. Out of all of our Malbecs, Adrianna is the one that takes the most time to soften and has the highest acidity. But after a few years in the bottle, it explodes in the nose and the palate. Only time will tell how it will age over the decades.

The Chardonnay from Adrianna is the core of Catena Alta Chardonnay, with cool-climate mineral notes and stone-fruit aromatics that are enhanced by sunlight. The Pinot Noir at Adrianna, the only truly varietal-tasting and -smelling Pinot Noir that I have been able to find in Mendoza, goes into my Luca Pinot Noir. There is a reason why people say that Pinot

Noir is the hardest grape to grow, but in a good year, the Dijon cuttings in Adrianna make my heart sing. The vineyard is named after my younger sister, Adrianna. During the early years of the winery, when I was in college, it was little Adrianna who cheered my father on when he had no idea if his Argentine quality quest would amount to anything. Her naming was inspired by the emperor Hadrian (my mother was reading *The Memoirs of Hadrian* when she was pregnant), one of the most forward-thinking and progressive emperors in ancient Rome.

Chapter IX:
THE SOUTHERN
UCO VALLEY: TUNUYÁN
AND SAN CARLOS

TUNUYÁN AND SAN CARLOS
At a Glance

Getting There: Drive directly south from Mendoza City on the Ruta 40; it's a 90 minute drive from Mendoza City and a 1-hour drive from the wineries in Luján de Cuyo.

Where to Go: Wineries (Clos de los Siete, Flechas de los Andes, Monteviejo, François Lurton, O. Fournier), vineyards, General San Martín museum at El Manzano Histórico, outdoor restaurants, fishing.

Wines/Varietals: Malbec, Syrah, Cabernet Sauvignon, Chardonnay.

Food: Locally grown peaches, apples, walnuts, almonds, quince, corn, lettuce, cabbage, cauliflower, and tomatoes; home-raised chicken, pork, and baby goat; freshly caught river trout.

Climate: Nights are very cold here. At elevations from 3,000 to 4,000 feet (914 to 1,219 m) above sea level, this is one of the coolest wine regions in Mendoza.

TUNUYÁN and SAN CARLOS

Facing the Andes as they curve toward the southeast, Tunuyán and San Carlos have been fruit-and-vegetable farming communities going back to the eighteenth century. Because of the region's proximity to the mountains, the sandy and rocky topsoils are particularly shallow, well drained, and low in fertility. Today, cool climate and low-fertility soils are considered ideal for high-quality viticulture. Water and nutrients are scarce, forcing the plant to mature slowly and to "naturally" produce a small amount of very flavorful and concentrated grapes. And this is exactly what we, producers of holy-grail-quality Malbec, want. There was a time, however, during the wine crisis of the 1960s, when volume production became the Argentine wine industry's driving force, and Malbec was replaced in many areas by high-yielding Criolla grapes. This was a time when the less-productive soils of the southern Uco Valley were the least sought-after in Mendoza. Fortunately, the low worth of their vineyards is what prevented many of the local growers from selling their land, and today we find some of the most precious old-vine, multigenerational family-owned properties in this area.

The region has undergone a winery gold rush of sorts recently, with more than a half-dozen new wineries cropping up in the last decade, among them the François Lurton Winery—built by the Bordelais Lurton brothers, Jacques and François—and the Michel Rolland club of high-powered French families at Clos de los Siete.

In the mid-nineties, most vineyard owners in the Altamira district were local. Today, several of Mendoza's most important wineries own vineyards in the area, and the land prices have increased significantly. Winemaker and agronomist Luis Reginato, who oversees all of the Luca Winery growers, was raised in San Carlos. "I have always believed in the outstanding quality potential of Altamira and La Consulta in San Carlos," says Luis. "The yields here are naturally low, and Malbec ripens at the end of the season, with perfectly soft and sweet tannins. But now it is so expensive to buy land here that I wish we could go back to the old days."

The landscape is a patchwork of vineyards interspersed with tomato fields; olive trees; quince, apple, pear, and other orchards; and most of the farmworkers live in the area's small towns. The land and its bounty are passionately treasured in Tunuyán and La Consulta: The most important local festivals are the Fiesta Nacional del Oregano (National Oregano Festival) and the Fiesta del Tomate (Tomato Festival). Recently, a vocal group of local activists managed

to stop a large gold and copper mining development that had threatened to contaminate the area's water supply.

You can reach Tunuyán and San Carlos either by heading straight south down the Ruta 40 from Mendoza City or Luján de Cuyo, or by traveling due southeast from Tupungato, taking smaller roads and enjoying (or not!) the massaging rhythm of the bumpy *caminos de tierra* (dirt roads). Tunuyán is the most populated district in the Uco Valley, with more than forty-five thousand inhabitants. San Carlos, the southernmost district, has a population of thirty-one thousand.

The southern Uco Valley enjoys a significant amount of Argentine tourism, especially on weekends. A big attraction is El Manzano Histórico ("the Historic Apple Tree"), an apple tree cum museum that honors the Argentine-independence general, José de San Martín. Legend has it that on his way to defeating the Spaniards in Chile, San Martín rested with his troops beneath this historic apple tree. The general is thought to have derived inspiration from the shady tree and the idyllic surroundings of imported pine trees, native flora, and mighty condors (symbolizing freedom) circling above. El Manzano Histórico is part of a large natural reserve, with numerous hiking paths, pretty rock-filled fishing streams, and gorgeous mountain views.

The mountain climate, the snow-covered peaks in the background, the clear skies, and the many natural springs and small rivers give the area a pure, clean, Swiss Alps feel. Eco de los Andes, Argentina's most important mineral water, is drawn from a natural spring in Tunuyán that is fed by icy glacier waters.

Wineries by Design

The wineries in the southern Uco Valley, many of them foreign owned, have some of the most innovative architectural designs in Mendoza. Flechas de los Andes (owned by the Dassault/Edmond de Rothschild families) is the creation of Philip Duillet (the *Star Wars* art director). From the outside, it looks a bit like a postmodern luxury hotel in Santa Fe, New Mexico. The interior is decorated with floors and furniture custom-made in elaborate geometric wood patterns. Monteviejo, also in the Clos de los Siete enclave, is owned by the charismatic Catherine Péré-Vergé, who also owns the prestigious Château le Gay in Pomerol, France. Monteviejo is beautifully in sync with the landscape. The front has an imposing brick and glass façade. The back of the winery is lined from top to bottom by a flowing row of vineyards, which creates the optical illusion that the vineyards continue onto the slope of the Andes in the background. Farther south in Eugenio Bustos, the fantastic and idiosyncratic space-ship-shaped structure at Spaniard José Manuel Ortega's O. Fournier winery is the creation of the architectural team Bórmida & Yanzón (see Chapter 8). My brother Ernesto Catena's one-of-a-kind Tikal Vineyard "labyrinth of vines and Nakbé sparkling wine facility" is in Vista Flores (see page 136).

*José Manuel Ortega,
owner, O. Fournier*

Michel Rolland, the World's Most Famous Wine Consultant

Michel Rolland is a controversial figure in the world of wine, especially in France. He was, in my opinion, unjustly vilified in *Mondovino*—Jonathan Nossiter's film about the globalization of wine—as one of the globalizers. Nossiter implies that Rolland makes cookie-cutter industrial wines, when, in fact, his life's work has been to travel the globe in search of hidden gems. One of the jewels that he found was Argentine Malbec (disclaimer: Michel Rolland has no connection with any of my family's properties). I can understand some resentment from his French colleagues. Michel Rolland's great skills in winemaking and ability to find unique vineyard sites around the world have provided a formidable challenge to the hegemony of French wine. As an Argentine, I am thankful to

Michel Rolland

him for what he has done to promote the virtues of our beloved Malbec. In Argentina, Rolland's wines could not be more different. Just taste a Yacochuya and a Clos de los Siete side by side and you'll see. The first is very ripe, sweet, almost port-like; the Clos has the spicy black fruit "tipicity" (common traits that define the breed) of Tunuyán Malbec, and big, lush tannins. The wines are as different as they can be.

Michel Rolland consults for wineries all over the world, but he owns more land in Argentina than anywhere else. He is an incredibly talented winemaker, and there is no doubt in my mind that he has improved the quality of many domaines both in his native France and throughout the world. He consults for such prestigious estates as Harlan, Dalla Valle, Araujo, Château Pavie, Château l'Evangile, Quintessa, Clos Apalta, and Ornellaia, among others. He is as passionate a winemaker as you will ever find.

Today, Rolland consults for several wineries in Argentina, including the five at Clos de los Siete in Tunuyán, Mendoza; Yacochuya in Salta; and Bodega del Fin del Mundo in Neuquén. He talks about Malbec with a child-like glee: "It is a wine with personality, a wine that can have beautiful black fruit aromatics, complexity, sweet tannins, concentration . . . all that a great wine should have." Here is another wonderful quote by Rolland, from his book *Wines of Argentina*: "If there is anywhere a place that encompasses the perfect match of climate, soils, costs, human resources, and, above all, freedom for creativity and minimal bureaucracy to hinder the genuine development of a new and exceptional viticulture, that place is undoubtedly Argentina."

Eating and Sleeping in the Southern Uco Valley

You can easily spend two days in the Uco Valley, with an overnight at one of the simple cabins or bed-and-breakfasts, or at the luxurious Casa Antucura Winery Lodge. The lodge is the vision of Italian publisher Anne-Caroline Bianchieri, who has created an eclectic and colorful style for each room, with objects brought from all over the world. The lodge has splendid views of the Andes, as well as a swimming pool, an enormous library (Sigmund Freud's full works), a foosball table, and a decorative cow on the premises.

Two of my favorite restaurants in the area are La Posada del Jamón— an "everything pork" restaurant, where you can order any imaginable variation of *jamón*—and Almacén de Uco, which is on the way to El Manzano Histórico and only open on weekends or by special reservation during the week. Almacén de Uco does an outdoor *asado* with perfectly crunchy and lightly seasoned grilled vegetables and an assortment of local cheeses and charcuteries. In the back of the restaurant there is an animal farm and a miniature lake, where on weekends children play while their parents dine inside.

If you are in the mood for a romantic winery lunch, take the afternoon off and spend a couple of hours at Natalia Ortega's Urban restaurant inside the O. Fournier winery. The window-lined restaurant has views of the vineyards that make you feel like meditating or kissing, depending on the company, and Natalia's beautifully prepared and locally sourced dishes have a way of making you ask for dessert even if you didn't intend to. The town that I most enjoy

in the Southern Uco Valley, La Consulta, located in San Carlos, is just a short drive from most of the wineries in Tunuyán. It has a pretty colonial plaza and a popular restaurant on the plaza, El Cielo, that serves fantastic daily specials. Local winemakers, farmers, and vineyard consultants of every rank make an obligatory stop at El Cielo every weekday for lunch.

Tikal Vineyard: Ernesto Catena's Vine Labyrinth

My brother, Ernesto, never ceases to surprise me. He is one of the most creative and charismatic people I know. When Ernesto told me he was building a "vine labyrinth" (a maze) in his Tikal vineyard, hoping that people would get lost and "get to know their inner souls" through hours spent finding the exit under the intense Mendozan sun, I had a hard time imagining the end result. The vineyard is now fully grown, and every time I go there, the experience is different. My brother is right when he says that the maze reveals people's true personalities.

At harvest time, Ernesto invites his friends and a crew of artists to pick the grapes and eat a bountiful *asado* until only a nap can save them. The Tikal vineyard is also home to one of the area's three polo fields. Winemakers

Ernesto Catena

and local players of all ages can be seen *taqueando* (hitting the ball) on the field during weekend tournaments. If you don't ride, you can spend the afternoon playing bocce ball at Tikal vineyard's own private court. Across the playing fields lies Nakbé, Ernesto's sparkling winery. Its architectural style is based on an ancient Mayan city Ernesto and his wife Joanna visited while traveling through Guatemala. In this winery, Ernesto makes the Almanegra sparkling rosé from the surrounding vineyards.

The beautifully manicured vineyard is planted with Malbec, Cabernet Sauvignon, and Cabernet Franc. Ernesto has degrees in computer science from Tufts University and design from the prestigious Domus Academy in Milan. He is both a scientist and an artist, a rare combination, but when it comes to wine, he is more artist than scientist. He either likes a wine or he doesn't, and if he doesn't like it he simply won't sell it. Plans are underway to open the Tikal maze to the public. Come and let yourself get lost.

PATAGONIA At a Glance

Getting There: The province of Neuquén is just south of Mendoza Province; the capital city of Neuquén is 400 miles (644 km) south of Mendoza City, and San Patricio del Chañar, Neuquen's main viticultural region, is a 45-minute drive from Neuquén city and the airport. The Río Negro province is farther southeast, and its viticultural region near General Roca is a 90-minute drive from Neuquén city and airport. The best way to get to Neuquén is to fly from Buenos Aires (LAN; 2-hour flight) to Neuquén city. If you are already in the well-known Patagonian towns of San Martín de Los Andes or Bariloche (there are direct flights from Buenos Aires to both cities, which are located in the southwestern part of Neuquén), it's a 4- to 6-hour drive to Neuquén and Río Negro's vineyards and wineries.

Where to Go: San Patricio del Chañar wineries and restaurants in Neuquén province; Río Negro province vineyards and wineries near General Roca.

Wines/Varietals: Malbec, Merlot, Cabernet Sauvignon, and Pinot Noir.

Food: Venison, lamb, freshwater trout; apples and pears; cured meats and fish; chocolate; cheese fondue.

Climate: Dry and much windier than in Mendoza. Temperatures fluctuate widely from day to night. The wine country altitudes are much lower than those in Mendoza, around 1,200 feet above sea level, as opposed to Mendoza's 3,000- to 5,000-foot (914- to 1,524-m) elevation. But the climate is still relatively cool—similar to Luján de Cuyo in Mendoza—due to the area's southern latitude. Farther southeast, in Río Negro, temperatures are somewhat lower due to the influence of the Río Negro ("Black River"), and that explains why cool-climate varietals such as Merlot and Pinot Noir can thrive here.

The Patagonian Wine Country: A Desert Oasis

Mention the name Patagonia to an adventurer, sportsman, or nature-lover, and watch him get all misty with thoughts of adorable penguins, beautiful mountain vistas, and a primal urge to get back to nature. Patagonia does have all these things, but keep in mind that the region comprises a group of provinces 1¼ times the size of Texas. The Patagonian wine country does not lie in the part of the region that is filled with picturesque snow-capped mountains and scented pine trees. Instead, Patagonian wineries thrive mainly in an oasis in the desert regions of the Neuquén and Río Negro Provinces, the center of much of Argentina's fruit production. If you are going to San Martín de Los Andes for fly-fishing or to hike in its beautiful backcountry, rent a car and drive to Neuquén (four hours), and you will have visited one of the most up-and-coming wine regions in the world, where some of Argentina's new rising stars are produced.

There were some early plantings in the Río Negro area in the late 1800s, but the serious era of viticulture started here in the early twentieth century with the arrival of European immigrants. By the 1960s, the area had become an important producer of wine, with some 44,460 acres (18,000 hectares) under vine in Río Negro and Neuquén, mostly planted under the *parral* pergola system. Vintners grew fine varietals such as Merlot, Malbec, Pinot Noir, Cabernet Sauvignon, Sauvignon Blanc, and Semillon, as well as the more productive table grape Criolla.

In the 1970s and 1980s, viticulture in Argentine Patagonia (Patagonia is divided between Chile and Argentina) suffered a fate similar to that of Mendoza: Many of the fine varietals were uprooted or grafted with lesser, more productive types, and volume replaced quality on a grand scale. All that would change in another decade.

Neuquén and San Patricio del Chañar

As you drive from the Neuquén desert through a valley of dry brush and sandy soil, a group of winery complexes known as San Patricio del Chañar appears seemingly out of nowhere. In the late 1990s, a handful of entrepreneurs (with the help of the Neuquén government) created this brand-new center of viticulture, which today includes several important wineries and mega-state-of-the-art wine facilities such as Bodega del Fin del Mundo, NQN, and Familia Schroeder. The viticultural climate here is ideal: The dry air prevents vineyard pests, and soils are alluvial and low in fertility. One problem for area

viticulturalists is the fierce winds. The arrival of strong winds during bud break can cause tremendous damage. To minimize the effects of wind, most wineries plant trees flanking the vineyards. Irrigation tubing must be placed right on top of the soil; if it's higher—as in Mendoza and other parts of the world—the water is simply blown away.

When Dinosaurs Walked the Earth
Argentine Patagonia is dinosaur country, home to the mighty creatures that roamed the earth millions of years ago. In fact, several bones of a giant Titanosaur were found at Familia Schroeder while the land was being prepared for planting. Titanosaurs were some of the heaviest dinosaurs on the planet, weighing up to 110 tons. In their honor, two wine lines at the winery have been named Saurus, and the Titanosaur fossils are on display in a small museum at the winery.

Fin del Mundo
One of my favorite stories is how Bodega del Fin del Mundo was named. Apparently, the owner, Julio Viola, was telling a well-known female winemaker from France about his new project in Patagonia. When he described the location, she protested, *"¡Pero eso es en el fin del mundo!"* Translation: "But that is at the end of the world!" And a winery name was hatched.

Río Negro
Río Negro is the older and more traditional viticultural area in Patagonia. One of the oldest wineries in the area, Humberto Canale, is where Hans Vinding-Diers—winemaker and part owner of the Noemia Winery—first made wine in Argentina. Another project worth mentioning is Infinitus, belonging to the wife/husband team of Diane and Hervé Joyaux Fabre, from Mendoza's Fabre Montmayou Winery. The couple were early comers to Río Negro and are making some very serious red blends with Malbec, Cabernet Sauvignon, and Merlot.

Two of the most exciting wineries in Río Negro—intensely boutique projects involving old-vine wines—are owned by Italians from renowned European winemaking families. The Noemia Winery is a project of Noemi Cinzano, the Italian countess of Cinzano (of the Argiano wine estate), who fell in love with the area, and Dutch winemaker Hans Vinding-Diers, who has made Patagonia his home. Chacra is owned by Piero Incisa della Roccheta (whose grandfather founded the Sassicaia wine estate). These celebrated wine personalities have joined the Argentines in Neuquén to help generate excitement about this remote part of the world. At Noemia, it is all about old-vine Malbec. At Chacra, the old-vine Pinot Noir is made in very small quantities and is pricey, but my sampling suggests that Piero is definitely on to something.

Many of the local wineries and vineyards were in poor condition until recently, when strong sales of Argentine wine allowed them to update their equipment. It would be unjust, however, to criticize the locals for not investing more in their vineyards and facilities. The reality is that Argentina has undergone one financial crisis after another, and credit is almost nonexistent, unless it comes through a government initiative.

Hans Vinding-Diers and Noemi Cinzano

Hans Vinding-Diers, Dutch Winemaker

Hans Vinding-Diers first came to Argentina as a consultant for the Humberto Canale winery, where he worked from 1998 to 2002 making special wines for the English market under a label named Black River: a reserve Malbec, Merlot, and Pinot Noir. After Hans met Noemi, countess of Cinzano, they began to look for an old-vine Malbec vineyard. They discovered Don Pirris's Mainque vineyard (planted circa 1932), which had been long abandoned but still produced grapes with incredible concentration and personality. Noemia, the winery they built around these old-vine grapes, is a small wooden house in the midst of a Tuscan garden designed by the countess. Hans Vinding-Diers

BODEGA
DEL FIN DEL MUNDO
PATAGONIA

Malbec

Chacra 123 / Cuadro 7

Año de Plantación 2.003

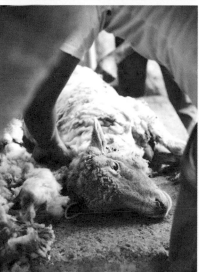

has truly embraced Argentina as his home, turning these special wines into his life's work. Today, the wines at Noemia are routinely among the highest-ranked Argentine wines in major publications worldwide. Although their history is relatively short, the wines have a rich heritage, one drawn from the lifeblood of these old vineyards.

Bodega Chacra and Old-Vine Pinot Noir

Pinot Noir is the delicate grape that has defined refinement in the world of wine. I started making Luca Pinot Noir in 1999 from French cuttings originally planted by my father at almost 5,000 feet (1,524 m) elevation in Tupungato, Mendoza. The first year we made the wine in small plastic bins by hand, not knowing exactly what we were doing. It is not an easy varietal to make; the berries and the aromas are so fragile that the wine can turn from glorious to dull without the winemaker ever knowing what happened. And if a Pinot Noir is not perfectly delicate and true to the varietal, it can be downright awful. Malbec, on the other hand, is more forgiving. I had only heard of Piero Incisa della Rocchetta's Pinot Noir Chacra when an Italian friend gave me a bottle to taste. What a surprise! It was pure Pinot Noir perfume, with nice acidity and delicate flavors.

The charming and unassuming Piero, grandson of the most-famous-in-all-of-Tuscany winemaker Mario Incisa della Rocchetta, the founder of Sassicaia, would say that it is all about the special *terroir* of this small lot of eighty-year-old vines that barely produce one pound per plant. Here is the story in his own words:

> In 2001, over the course of a dinner with Noemi Cinzano and Hans Vinding-Diers, I had a rare experience. I tasted a wine that I immediately fell in love with. Its characteristics were familiar, yet I was completely fooled by its geographical origin—I thought it was from Burgundy but it was actually made in Patagonia.
>
> I persuaded the owner to rent the vineyard to me for one year, and we made Chacra Treinta y Dos (so named for the year—1932—when the vineyard was planted), our first vintage in vat No. 7 at Bodega Noemia. I convinced the owner to sell the land to me in 2004, and the next year I bought the neighboring farm, which had Pinot Noir vineyards that were planted in 1955.
>
> Today, at our own winery at Chacra, we have a traditional artisanal approach to winemaking. We do pretty much everything by

Piero Incisa della Rocchetta

hand— we prune, harvest, and de-stem by hand; we vinify without machinery or steel; and most of the time we decant by gravity. Chacra is not a conventional business; it's a passion, a personal folly. In Italy, our wineries and estates have belonged to my family for a long time. Tenuta San Guido, where Sassicaia was born, has been in my family for some nine hundred years—and the historical trajectory is embedded in the family DNA. I view our role there as one of guardians preserving the business to hand over to the next generation. This leaves little room for ego or new experiments. At Chacra, however, we have the luxury to start from nothing, which gives us great flexibility and freedom and no ties to preconceived notions or concepts. Our goal is to keep producing single-vineyard biodynamic wines that are of consequence, as we believe that our *terroir* is capable of yielding wines that are unique in character.

Chapter XI:
SALTA

SALTA At a Glance

Getting There: Salta is located in the northernmost tip of Argentina, a 2-day bus ride from Mendoza. I recommend that you fly from Buenos Aires to Salta City (a 1-hour flight) and then drive from Salta City airport to Cafayate or Colomé.

Where to Go: The valley of Cafayate is located about a 4-hour (186-mile/300-km) drive southwest of Salta City. Colomé, Donald and Ursula Hess's property, is located between Salta City and Cafayate (it's a 4½-hour drive from Salta City, because you are going on dirt roads for part of the way), so you can go to Colomé on the way to Cafayate or on your way back.

Wines/Varietals: Torrontés and Malbec.

Food: Salta is the best place to experience Native Argentine cuisine: pumpkin, corn, bell peppers; spicy vegetable, bean, and meat stews; artisanal goat cheeses; the famous Salteña empanadas.

Climate: The climate in Salta is generally warmer than in Mendoza because of its northern latitude. In the high-altitude areas over 6,000 feet (1,824 m) in elevation, however, the climate is as cool as in some areas of high-altitude Mendoza. The surrounding hills provide respite from the intense high-altitude sun. Remember: In South America, north is warmer; south is cooler. So when you travel north, you will need to go to a higher elevation to find a cooler climate.

The Slow Argentina

In Salta, every road is curving, and every few miles the landscape seems to change from one sort of geological formation and color to another. On the way to Colomé, for example, you pass different kinds of rock formations, from the sharp, almost knifelike *agujas* (needles) to multicolored mountains to red mountains. Then the cacti take over.

Salta is the province where the Argentine version of Andean music comes from, which is played with a tiny guitar—*el charango*—and the Andean flute, made of eight dried-up sugarcanes attached together. It's a place where vineyards are lined with hills and cacti, and wild goats and horses share the streets with pedestrians and old cars. Everything in Salta is touched by poetry or derived from a legend. The Native culture is prevalent, and there is a dreaminess and sense of spirituality here that I have felt elsewhere only in places like Nepal or the Tibetan Himalayas.

The pace is slower in Salta than in Argentina's wine capital, Mendoza, and things move at a snail's pace compared to Buenos Aires. It's no wonder that Salta is known as "the slow Argentina," where it can take forty-five minutes to get a beer at a bar (because the owner is watching a soccer game on TV) or a whole afternoon to move a cow sitting in the middle of the road. Here, being in a hurry is simply not tolerated.

Cafayate

Cafayate, Salta's wine capital, is located 186 miles (300 km) south of Salta City and its main airport. Cafayate is one of several Chachaquí valleys in the region. Located at approximately 6,000 feet (1,824 m) in elevation, 200 miles (321 km) south of the Tropic of Capricorn, Cafayate is flanked by mountains on all sides. Its vineyards benefit from the shade and the cool, dry nights characteristic of this high semi-desert valley.

The Incans arrived in Salta from Peru in the 1480s, the Spanish conquistadors in 1535. The local Natives, descendants of the Incans, waged battle with the Spaniards for many decades, and this, people say, led to the origin of the word *calchaquí: calcha* ("rebel") and *quí* ("the very")—"the valleys of the very rebellious." They must have kept the Spaniards at bay for quite some time: The names of the towns—Cafayate, Cachi, Anastaco, and Guachapas—are more indigenous than Spanish, and the features of the people are more Indian than those in Mendoza.

If you have a few days to spare, I recommend you tour the Calchaquí Valley circuit, which includes the seventeenth-century town of Molinos, with its adobe and mud houses, and its nearby vicuña nursery (a vicuña poncho sells for about 3,000 U.S. dollars; the animal can be shorn only every three years). The Parque Nacional de los Cardones houses 162,5000 acres (65,000 hectares) of gigantic cardón cacti, which are 250 to 300 years old and grow 6.5 to 10 feet (2 to 3 m) high.

Arriving in Cafayate is dramatic, no matter which direction you come from. If you fly to Salta from Buenos Aires (there are no other direct connections) and drive south for 186 miles (300 km), a four-hour drive, you start your journey in a tropical forest of palms and banana trees, and lush tropical gardens. After you pass the mountain range, where the rains stop, all of a sudden you find yourself in a valley area flanked by mountains, cacti, and brush. Goat and donkey herds run in and out of the small streets and even highways. You get a strong feeling that you've time-traveled to the past.

Another, more adventurous journey is to take the fifteen-hour drive north from Mendoza and watch the dramatic change in scenery. In Mendoza, the snow-capped Andes provide a distant backdrop, and state-of-the-art wineries, vineyards, and orchards are omnipresent. In the north, the winding roads are lined with hillside villages and mud houses. Scattered cows, goats, and other animals roam about. Here, people walking home with their groceries or carrying goods on a donkey cart may make you feel as if globalization will never make it to this corner of the world. The town of Cafayate is better kept than most of the small surrounding towns, and it is accustomed to local and foreign tourism. The town has a pottery factory, an artisanal market, a basket-weaving workshop, and a few wineries. Nevertheless, this is still "slow Argentina," with the rhythms of an old-fashioned, more leisurely way of life. Cafayate offers several hostels and hotels, including the very old and luxed-up Patios de Cafayate, situated in a beautiful colonial home that was previously owned by the Michel Torino wine family and is now a Starwood resort. It's been completely refurbished with period furniture and has a fabulous solar-panel-heated pool and a wine spa where you can get a grapeseed oil massage or a grapeseed rub.

The Wineries of Salta

I've heard many different versions of how fine wine was introduced to Salta. My favorite one, told to me by Colomé Winery's Donald Hess, traces it back to the daughter of the last Spanish governor. She was studying in Paris, it seems, and brought back vines from the Bordeaux region at her father's request. And so it

goes: For almost everything in Salta there is a legend that explains why things are the way they are, from the local geography to the architecture.

Most of the well-known wineries are within ten minutes of Cafayate, including Felix Lavaque, El Esteco, Etchart, San Pedro de Yacochuya, and Bodega Jose L. Mounier. Torrontés is the grape varietal that rules the roost here, although the region's high altitude makes it an excellent location for Malbec as well. At several wineries, when we asked why Torrontés from Salta is so aromatic, we were told: "Everything is aromatic here, the fruits, the vegetables, the spices, the flowers, and of course the wines."

The Torrontés Varietal

Tom Canavan, a United Kingdom wine expert, once described the exuberant Muscat-like aromas of Torrontés: "Pulling the cork on a Torrontés can be like opening a bottle of eau de cologne." With all the floral and peach aromatics, you might expect Torrontés to be a sweet wine. Instead, the flavors are crisp and dry, but with an unctuousness and slight minerality that coat your whole mouth and tongue and make you want a second sip. It's a perfect appetizer wine, a perfect cheese wine, and a perfect by-itself wine.

Argentina grows and produces three kinds of Torrontés: Torrontés Riojano, Torrontés Sanjuanino, and Torrontés Mendocino. Currently, there are about 21,500 acres (8,700 hectares) of Torrontés Riojano and 11,860 acres (4,800 hectares) of Torrontés Sanjuanino planted in Argentina; it is in fact the most widely planted white varietal in the country. Although only 1 percent of Argentina's Torrontés is grown in Cafayate, this small town-district is considered the best place to plant the varietal because of its very cold nights— it is located at an altitude of over 5,600 feet (1,707 m)—and very sunny days. Torrontés is susceptible to sunburn, so most vineyards are planted in the *parral* (high pergola) training system, which keeps some of the sunlight away and maintains an area of coolness around the maturing clusters.

I have heard different opinions about what the yields should be for Torrontés. Some winemakers seem to prefer relatively high yields, because at the time of harvest—which is fairly early in the season, in February—acidity is greater in higher-yielding vineyards and the style is crisper. Other winemakers prefer lower-yielding old vines. I have tasted good wines made using both techniques. There is also the question of style: oxidative (letting oxygen in) versus protective (not allowing in much oxygen by keeping the wine in cooled stainless-steel tanks). Most people today prefer the protective style, which gives the wine fruitier and more floral aromas, and a crisper mouthfeel.

Some wineries have attempted to attract consumers by making their Torrontés sweeter, but most of the well-known producers are making their Torrontés dry. Some of the best Torrontés bottlings are made by Alamos, Crios, Mounier, Lavaque, Yacochuya, Etchart, Michel Torino, and Tilia.

For many years, people thought that Argentine Torrontés had originated in the Galicia region of Spain, where there is a varietal with the same name. In 2003, a group of brilliant researchers at Argentina's Institute of Viticulture, in conjunction with UC Davis's professor and wine producer Carole Meredith, answered this question in the *Journal of Enology and Viticulture*. It is now thought to be virtually impossible that the obscure Torrontés grape from Spain is the same as the Argentine Torrontés. These researchers identified Argentina's Torrontés Riojano and Sanjuanino as the progeny of a cross between the Mediterranean grape Muscat of Alexandria and Criolla Chica ("Little Criolla"). The latter is a small pink grape (a member of the same family as the Mission grape) used for table wines in Argentina. What's most interesting is that Torrontés Mendocino (the kind of Torrontés generally found in Mendoza) was found to be a completely unrelated varietal. This might be part of the explanation why the Torrontés Riojano (Rioja is the province immediately south of Salta, which also grows Torrontés) that is grown in Salta produces such a different—and better—wine.

The supposed "father" of Torrontés is Muscat of Alexandria, a member of the Muscat family that surprisingly does not make very aromatic wines. The versions of Muscat of Alexandria that I have tasted from Greece, however, do have the same kind of richness in the palate that I enjoy in Salta's Torrontés. What I love about the "father" of Torrontés is that experts consider it an ancient vine and one of the oldest varietals still in existence—apparently Cleopatra liked to drink it. Criolla Chica, the "mother" of Torrontés, was the pink grape used by the Catholic priests to make sacramental wine. (The priests first arrived in the sixteenth century to convert the Natives and stayed until Argentina gained independence from Spain in the early nineteenth century.) Torrontés Riojano (the variety grown in Salta) most likely originated in Argentina from a cross between these two grapes—making it the only native Argentine varietal with important acreage in our country.

José Luis Mounier: A Mendozan Turned Torrontés Master

The Mounier winery Finca las Nubes, located in a small mountain valley, is as quaint and romantic as any place I have ever been. Señora Mounier is your tour guide, and the barrel room is right next to the manual labeling table. José

Luis Mounier started his own project after working at Etchart for twenty years and is considered the foremost expert in Torrontés in the region. José Luis grew up and went to school in Mendoza, where his immigrant French grandparents taught him to love and respect vines and wine. He paid his own way through school, taking any job that would come his way—harvesting peaches and grapes, sewing clothes, doing construction—while his mother worked as a maid because she had vowed to support the family so that her children could go to school. In her own words: "If you don't study, you will never amount to anything." Today, José Luis is a consultant for Lavaque winery, and he has taken Torrontés to its highest level. His Torrontés is to die for. Torrontés is a really delicious aromatic white, but it is delicate and not easy to make in a fresh, fruity, mineral style. José Luis Mounier is a master at this.

José Luis Mounier

San Pedro de Yacochuya

Another project worth seeing is San Pedro de Yacochuya, a partnership between the Etchart family and the famed French wine consultant Michel Rolland. The Torrontés here is aromatic and crisp, and the Yacochuya red is deep, high in alcohol, and very, very lush. The business is a family affair. Marcos Etchart is the winemaker; his wife and mother arrange meals for guests (they need one day's notice); and his father, Arnaldo, reads and lectures about northern Argentine poetry.

Arnaldo Etchart

Arnaldo Etchart is what I call a classic. His daily "uniform" consists of a cow-boy hat, a gaucho vest and scarf, long white hair, a striped tailored shirt, and a leather vest. One might confuse him with a gaucho, except that gauchos don't wear tailored shirts and don't grow their white hair long below their shoulders; he is simply Arnaldo Etchart. "If you don't read poetry," Arnaldo famously said to my friend, winemaker Fernando Buscema, "your wines will taste like caca, you hear me, young man?" Instead of a business card, Arnaldo hands out his poetry lecture notes and a few poems about wine from his favorite poet, Jaime Davalos. His son, Marcos, says "My father is *loco* (crazy)." But this "crazy" man has managed to be known by all as the person to see for wine-related business in Salta. Although he sold his namesake winery Etchart to Pernod Ricard in 1996, he still owns the gorgeous Yacochuya vineyard and winery jointly with his wife and children and winemaker Michel Rolland (Arnaldo was ridiculed in the wine documentary *Mondovino* for professing adoration for Rolland). Arnaldo's home—an old adobe house with views of a gorgeous waterfall from its indoor patio—is adjacent to the winery.

I don't know if Mr. Etchart is right in his belief that better wine can be made while reading poetry, but I tend to agree with him that we would all ben-efit from a bit more poetry in our lives. And this free-spirited man, with his long white hair, poetry, and rambling speeches, is right in tune with the dreaminess of Salta Province.

Nacimiento del Vino

Como un toro frutal, el mosto herido
se revuelca en las cubas resollando,
y entre canciones sórdidas va ahogando
en soledad su cálido balido

The Birth of Wine

Like a toro-bull made of fruit, the injured wine juice
tumbles in the bins crying out loud,
and in between hopeless songs,
it drowns in the solitude of a warm roar.

—*Jaime Davalos*

Colomé

The crown jewel of Salta is the Colomé of Donald and Ursula Hess. Well known in the United States as one of Napa's early pioneers, the Swiss engineer and his wife fell in love with Colomé and decided to turn this remote and stunningly beautiful place into their spiritual home. Donald Hess told me that he came to Salta three times before he found a way to arrive at Colomé. The river was flooded the first two years, so he couldn't make it through. But once the Hesses saw the one-bedroom vestiges of the Colomé winery, they made up their mind that they would turn Colomé into one of Argentina's most important wineries.

Randle Johnson, the Hess properties' winemaking chief, told me that after two years of waging battle to bring water and electricity up the rocky, three-hour road to Colomé, he tried many times to persuade the Hesses to sell the land and give up on this project. But anyone who meets Donald Hess knows that this man does not give up—ever. He showed me his thirteen-thousand-kilowatt electricity generator, which gets its energy from a river up the mountain. When Mr. Hess asked the Salta governor if he could do such a

Ursula and Donald Hess

thing, the governor flatly replied: "There are no rules against it, but I don't know of anyone who has done it or why anyone would want to do it." Some $1.2 million later, Mr. Hess admits the enterprise was difficult. "But we will never have to pay for electricity again," he says brightly.

Everything—the inn, its lavender and cactus gardens, the museum, the tasting room—is done in the local adobe style by local architects with Donald's input. The Hesses have vowed to transform their winery into a mecca for art, meditation, and wine. For Ursula, however, it is what Colomé has done for the local community that matters most. She has set up a hotel school and an elementary school. Donald Hess proudly tells me that the Colomé soccer team recently won the local league competition. Prior to their arrival, the four-hundred-person Colomé community—living in shantytown-like huts scattered around the mountains—had been riven by malnutrition and alcoholism and faced an uncertain future. The people lived in dire poverty and had extremely limited access to food, medical care, and education. For the Hesses, providing this community with a place of work and refuge has been their proudest achievement.

But their wines are an achievement too. The wines of Colomé, especially the Torrontés and Malbec, have a *terroir*-based style that is reproduced in every vintage. The Torrontés is crisp and aromatic. The Malbec is ripe, intensely aromatic and velvety on the palate.

Chapter XII:
TOURING BUENOS AIRES
AND THE ARGENTINE
WINE COUNTRY

Bustling Cities and Wide-open Spaces

Almost half of Argentina's population of 40 million lives in and around the capital of Buenos Aires. In a country that comprises more than a million square miles (2.6 million square km)—it's the second-largest country in South America and the eighth-largest country in the world—this means that the outer provinces are relatively underpopulated and enjoy plenty of wide-open spaces. In fact, when visiting Argentina's wine-producing provinces, it's easy to imagine a time when gauchos and horse-drawn carriages roamed the streets. Provincial Argentines revere their peace and quiet just as much as Porteños— the name given to people from Buenos Aires and derived from the word *puerto* ("port")—relish their more chaotic and worldly surroundings. This book highlights the main viticultural regions of Argentina: Mendoza—where 70 percent of Argentine wine is made—Salta, and Patagonia. But if you want to truly understand Argentine wine and food, I suggest that you spend some time in the bustling city of Buenos Aires. This is where you will see the greatest creativity in food and design. Porteños pride themselves on their cultural heritage, their museums, their Parisian-style vintage architecture, and their fashionable cafes and restaurants.

In Mendoza, Salta, and Patagonia, you will see how Argentines have transformed, in less than a decade, an aging and outdated industry— winemaking—into Argentina's most visible export: dark and tasty Malbec wine.

But Argentina has a few other important wine-growing provinces, mainly the provinces that line the Andes from Neuquén in the south to Salta in the north. Here, the climate is dry and warm (but not too warm), and the provinces include, from Mendoza northward: San Juan, La Rioja, and Catamarca, immediately south of Salta. The San Rafael region in southeastern Mendoza, about a four-hour drive from Mendoza City, has several high-quality producers, such as Familia Bianchi, Familia Roca, and Lavaque, that are worth visiting, especially if you have your own car and time on your hands. San Juan follows Mendoza in wine production volume. Although San Juan has traditionally been known for its inexpensive table wines, the province has several high-altitude valleys that are capable of producing highly concentrated and interesting Cabernet Sauvignon, Malbec, and Syrah. The high-altitude valleys of San Juan and La Rioja (to the north of San Juan) are places to watch in the next decade.

It is easy to fall in love with Argentina and its people. Argentines are industrious, creative, passionate, and hardworking. But there is also a dark side to Argentina, which comes from a long history of unstable politics and economics. Perhaps it is this instability that makes our people so passionate. It is rare to find an Argentine who saves his or her money. The thought is "Why save it?" when tomorrow an exchange-rate crisis or a government bank freeze could make it all disappear overnight.

Down Argentina Way: Savvy Travel Tips

In the last decade, tourism has boomed in Argentina and the country has become one of the world's top wine-producing and winemaking countries. Here are some tips for travelers to Argentina:

A kiss on the cheek: In Argentina, it's customary to greet a friend with a single kiss on the right cheek. Most Argentines know that foreigners shake hands upon greeting and will do so accordingly, but if you kiss an Argentine on the cheek the first time you meet her, she will not be surprised. It is also common for a man to greet his brother, father, or close friend with a kiss on the cheek.

Asking for directions: In the wine country, people are always happy to give directions—which, alas, are often wrong. I suggest you buy an ACA (Automobil Club Argentino) map as soon as you get here, or preferably hire a driver.

Bargaining: Haggling is okay at outdoor flea markets, but in stores or shopping malls, don't try to bargain unless you are paying with cash instead of a credit card, for which most vendors will give you a discount.

Counterfeit money: Beware of counterfeit money. Try to pay taxis with exact (or close to exact) change.

Drinking: Public drunkenness is frowned upon in Argentina, so if you are out at a bar or a restaurant and drink too much, I suggest you retire to your hotel and sleep it off. Or pace yourself and drink lots of water and eat lots of food with your wine or your Fernet and Coke (Argentina's most popular drink).

Insider hotel rates: Some hotels have rates for Argentines and entirely different rates for foreigners, so if you have an Argentine friend or contact who can make a reservation for you, it might save you some money.

Ordering steak: Old-fashioned Argentines such as myself like their steak well done, but after a decade of heavy tourism, Argentines know that most foreigners prefer their beef rare. So if you like your meat rare, simply order *jugoso* (juicy), and you will get what you want. If you want it medium-rare, ask for *a punto*.

Tipping: Gratuities are generally smaller in Argentina than in the United States, but Argentines welcome the extra tips from foreigners. Fifteen percent is a generous restaurant tip. Taxicab drivers are not used to getting tips, so they are grateful for any gratuity.

Argentina Luxury Wine Itinerary

The following are my suggestions for an ideal holiday in Argentina's wine country.

Days 1 and 2: Fly into Buenos Aires. Stay in a hotel that fits your budget or rent an apartment. I would recommend staying in Palermo (trendy), Recoleta (traditional and safest), or Centro (downtown). Have an *asado* at Las Lilas in Puerto Madero. Dine on Fernando Trocca's fabulous New Argentine cuisine at Sucre, which has an extensive wine list full of old vintages. Visit the colorful port town of La Boca and dine at Francis Mallmann's Patagonia Sur. Stroll leisurely through the Recoleta cemetery, the Bellas Artes museum, and the trendy Palermo Soho (keep an eye on your wallet or purse).

Days 3 and 4: Take the early flight to Mendoza, and spend two nights at one of the downtown hotels while visiting nearby wineries in Maipú and Luján de Cuyo. I recommend hiring a car with a driver, which costs about the same as renting your own car and makes wine tasting safer and a lot more fun. Your hotel can help you with the arrangements.

Days 5 and 6: Move to the Cavas Wine Lodge in Luján de Cuyo, or to one of the posadas or lodges in the Uco Valley, and spend two days visiting wineries in the Uco Valley.

Days 7, 8, and 9: Take the Andesmar bus (ideally, in first class) from Mendoza City to Salta, or fly back to Buenos Aires and catch a transfer to Salta and spend two days at Colomé or Cafayate, Salta. You can also take an Andesmar bus to Neuquén City from Mendoza on your way to Patagonia.

Days 10, 11, and 12: Fly back from Salta to Buenos Aires and catch the two-hour flight to Bariloche, Patagonia, and if you can, stay at the Llao Llao Hotel. Enjoy the mountains and forests for a day or two, then rent a car and head to the wine country in Neuquén and Río Negro (a five-hour drive from Bariloche).

Days 13 and 14: Fly back to Buenos Aires from Neuquén city and rest in the capital city before heading home.

Laura Catena's Buenos Aires Favorites

Here are some of my favorite restaurants and bars in Buenos Aires:

For a Typical Asado

San Telmo: La Brigada—white tablecloths, a traditional and phenomenal wine list

Palermo Soho: Minga, La Cabrera

Puerto Madero: Cabaña Las Lilas, La Caballeriza

Palermo: La Dorita

Las Cañitas: La Caballeriza

Plaza San Martín: Plaza Grill at the 100-year-old Marriott Plaza Hotel

Recoleta: La Cabaña

Innovative Argentine Cuisine

Palermo Viejo: Casa Cruz

Belgrano Chico: Sucre

Centro: Tomo I

Palermo Hollywood: Tegui

International Cuisine and Trendy Places to Watch Fashionable People

Palermo Hollywood: Osaka, Libelula for Japanese/Peruvian cuisine

Palermo Hollywood: El Green Bamboo for phenomenal Thai food and deadly drinks

Palermo Soho: Bereber for Moroccan food

Palermo: Astrid y Gaston for Japanese/Peruvian food

La Boca: Il Matterello for Italian food, Patagonia Sur for Francis Mallmann's creations in a beautifully restored colonial house

Oviedo Restaurant Chef and Owner

Barrio Norte: Oviedo for the best fish and shellfish in Buenos Aires

Recoleta: La Bourgogne for French food

Late-Night Lounges

Puerto Madero: The Faena Hotel, for a Thursday-night cabaret and a mixed foreign and Argentine crowd

Palermo Viejo: Congo Bar

Palermo: Bar 878

Costanera (by the river): Pacha, for dancing and electronic music

Centro (downtown): Café Tortoni, for traditional French décor and tango shows

Centro: Gran Bar Danzon, for varied drinks and excellent people-watching

Tango

Barracas near La Boca port: Señor Tango, for a good show

Palermo Viejo: La Viruta, where locals go to dance

RECIPES

Empanadas Salteñas 174

Carbonada 178

Milanesas 181

Rib-Eye Steak with Chimichurri
and Patagonian Potatoes 183

Venison with Berry Chutney,
Sweet Potatoes, and Caramelized Almonds 186

Crepes with Dulce de Leche 189

Alfajores de Maizena 192

Helado de Torrontés 195

Quince Dessert 197

EMPANADAS SALTEÑAS

The word *empanada*, derived from *pan* ("bread"), literally means "covered in bread" and refers to a stuffing wrapped in dough and either baked or fried. Depending on their South or Central American country of origin, empanadas have different fillings, ranging from corn or cheese to chicken, pork, or beef. It's believed that empanadas were brought to the New World by immigrants from Galicia in Spain. Empanada recipes are passed from mother to daughter in most Argentine families. There is always a secret trick or ingredient that is only revealed to a blood relative. Empanadas salteñas—from Salta province—are particularly flavorful because they are spicier than most other Argentine versions. Torrontés, the white wine typical of Salta, makes an unusually good pairing for the red-meat-filled Salta empanadas; the intense aromas and minerality of the wine marry beautifully with the juices and sweet raisins in the empanadas. Of course, Argentine Malbec and Cabernet Sauvignon are also a good pairing with meat empanadas, especially with the raisinless version that is typical of Mendoza.

   This recipe was given to me by Ursula Hess of Colomé Winery in Salta. Because it uses tenderloin rather than ground beef, it makes light, nongreasy empanadas.

FILLING

1 tbsp canola oil

1¼ cups/185 g finely chopped white onions

1 bay leaf

1 small red bell pepper/capsicum, seeded, deveined, and cut into ¼-in/6-mm dice

½ tsp salt

1 tsp red pepper flakes, or more to taste

1 small potato, peeled and cut into ½-in/12-mm dice

One 3-in-/7.5-cm-long piece of beef marrow bone

½ lb/230 g beef tenderloin cut into ¼-in/6-mm dice

½ cup/120 ml chicken or beef stock

1 tsp ground cumin

1 tsp sweet paprika

⅓ cup/85 g golden raisins/sultanas

¼ cup/35 g chopped pitted green olives

3 hard-cooked large eggs, coarsely chopped

2 tbsp dried bread crumbs

¼ cup/18 g finely sliced green/spring onions or finely chopped fresh chives

DOUGH

3 cups/385 g all-purpose/plain flour

½ cup/125 g cold lard or vegetable shortening

¾ cup/180 ml ice water

1 large egg beaten with 1 tsp milk

Makes about **2 DOZEN** empanadas

Preheat the oven to 350°F/180°C/gas 4.

For the filling: In a medium sauté pan or frying pan, heat the canola oil over medium heat and sauté the onions with the bay leaf until well browned, 8 to 10 minutes. Add the bell pepper/capsicum and sauté until soft, about 5 minutes. Add the salt and red pepper flakes and sauté for 2 minutes. Remove and discard the bay leaf and set the onions aside.

In a small saucepan of lightly salted water, simmer the potato until tender, about 15 minutes. Drain and set aside.

Place the marrow bone upright on a small baking dish and cover loosely with aluminum foil. Bake for 12 minutes. Remove from the oven and let cool to the touch, then scoop out the marrow, cut into ¼-in/6-mm dice, and set aside. Reserve the bone for your dog.

Put the tenderloin in a small saucepan. In a separate saucepan, bring the stock to a boil. Immediately pour the hot stock over the beef, stir in the diced marrow, and bring the mixture to a boil. Cover the pan, remove it from the heat, and let stand for 5 minutes. Add the onion mixture, cumin, and paprika. Gently stir in the potato. Let cool, then cover and refrigerate for at least 10 hours or overnight.

continued...

Fold in the raisins, olives, eggs, bread crumbs, and the green/spring onions or chives. Refrigerate until ready to form the empanadas.

For the dough: In a food processer, combine the flour and lard or shortening. Pulse until the mixture resembles a coarse meal. With the machine running, add just enough of the ice water to form the dough—it will come together in a clump.Transfer the dough to a lightly floured board and gently form into a 5-in/12-cm disk. Be careful not to overwork the dough, or it will become tough. Cover with a damp cloth and let rest for 30 minutes.

To form and bake the empanadas: Preheat the oven to 400°F/200°C/gas 6. Line 2 baking sheets/trays with parchment/baking paper.

Break off a walnut-sized piece of dough and roll into a 1-in/2.5-cm ball. Gently flatten. Using a rolling pin on a lightly floured board, roll the dough into a 5-in/12-cm round. Repeat, using all the dough. Place 2 tbsp filling in the center of each dough round. Moisten the edges of each dough round with the egg mixture (use a pastry brush or your finger), and gently fold the dough over, lining up the edges, to form a half-moon. Press the edges together with your fingers, then with the tines of a fork to seal the empanada. Transfer the empanadas to a prepared pan, placing them about 1½ in/4 cm apart. (To bake later, cover the empanadas and refrigerate for several hours until ready to bake.)

Brush the empanadas with the egg mixture. Bake for 12 to 15 minutes, or until nicely browned. Remove from the oven and let cool on the baking sheets— they're a little too fragile to move while hot. These empanadas are best served warm.

CARBONADA

Carbonada is a classic meat and vegetable stew that is typical of northern Argentina, Chile, and Peru. This version is from the Mendozan chef Lucas Bustos. It's his interpretation of an old recipe he learned from a grandmother in Tunuyán, Uco Valley. *Carbonada* from the north of Argentina generally has a sweet and sour component—derived from fruits—and is often spicy. Mendozans prefer their flavors simple and unadulterated by spice, as here. On a cold winter day, there is little more heartwarming than eating a *carbonada* by a well-lit fire. The fire serves the double purpose of cooking the *carbonada* and warming cold hands and feet. Serve this stew in a hollowed-out pumpkin—seeds, strings, and some of the flesh removed—for a traditional presentation.

6 cups/1.4 l vegetable stock

2 tbsp canola oil

1 lb/455 g flank steak, cut into ½-in/12-mm dice

2 small onions, julienned

1 red bell pepper/capsicum, seeded, deveined, and cut into ½-in/12-mm dice

3 garlic cloves, finely chopped

1 large or 2 small tomatoes, seeded and cut into ½-in/12-mm dice

2 tbsp finely chopped fresh oregano

1 bay leaf

1½ cups/360 ml Chardonnay

1 lb/455 g cooking pumpkin such as Baby Bear, or butternut squash, peeled, seeded, and cut into 1-in/2.5-cm cubes

Kernels cut from 2 ears corn (cobs reserved)

2 russet potatoes, peeled and cut into ½-in/12-mm dice

2 sweet potatoes, peeled and cut into ½-in/12-mm dice

2 tbsp salt (less if stock is already salted)

1 tsp freshly ground pepper

SERVES 6
as a main course

In a large nonreactive stockpot, bring the vegetable stock to a boil, add the corncobs, reduce the heat to low, and simmer for about 30 minutes.

In a heavy soup pot, heat the oil over high heat until shimmering. Add the flank steak and sauté until browned, about 5 minutes. Add the onions and sauté until golden, about 5 minutes. Add the bell pepper and garlic and sauté for 2 minutes. Add the tomatoes, oregano, and bay leaf, and continue cooking for 3 minutes more. Add the wine, bring to a boil, and cook for 5 minutes.

Remove the corncobs from the stock and add the stock to the pot. Add the pumpkin or squash, corn kernels, russet potatoes, and sweet potatoes and season with the salt and pepper. Bring to a boil, then reduce the heat and simmer for about 20 minutes, or until all the vegetables are tender but not falling apart. Taste and adjust the seasoning.

MILANESAS

Milanesas, breaded slices of beef or chicken, are the Argentine version of the American hamburger: a dish that all Argentine children and adults wish they could have every day for lunch and dinner. It is impossible to find a neighborhood restaurant in Argentina that doesn't serve *milanesas*. They are often eaten a day old in a bread sandwich—*sandwich de milanesa*—with mustard, mayonnaise, lettuce, and tomato. This recipe from my mother, Elena Catena, includes a milk marinade that she claims to be the secret to tender meat. The *napolitana* finish, with melted cheese and tomato on top, was my favorite as a child.

2 lb/910 g boneless top sirloin beef steaks, trimmed and cut into eight ¼-in-/6-mm-thick horizontal slices (ask the butcher to slice)

¾ cup/180 ml milk

3 large eggs

3 tbsp finely chopped fresh flat-leaf parsley

3 garlic cloves, finely chopped

1 tsp salt

½ tsp freshly ground pepper

3 cups/375 g dried bread crumbs

Canola oil for frying

Lemon wedges for serving

SERVES 8

In a medium bowl, combine the steak and milk. Refrigerate for 1 hour. Remove from the refrigerator.

In a shallow bowl, whisk together the eggs, parsley, garlic, salt, and pepper. On a large plate or platter, spread about 1 cup of the bread crumbs. Remove a slice of steak from the milk and allow it to drain. Dip the steak in the egg mixture, then press both sides into the bread crumbs. Repeat with the remaining slices until all are coated; add more bread crumbs to the plate as needed.

continued . . .

In a large sauté pan or frying pan, heat ½ in/12 mm oil over medium-high heat until shimmering. Cook each steak slice for 2 to 3 minutes per side. Using a slotted metal spatula, transfer the slice to paper towels/absorbent paper to drain. Keep warm in a low oven while frying the remaining slices.

Alternatively, the *milanesas* may be baked on a lightly oiled baking sheet/tray on an upper rack in a preheated 400°F/200°C/gas 6 oven. Cook until golden brown, 4 to 5 minutes on each side.

Serve at once, with lemon wedges.

Milanesas Napolitana: Place the browned slices on a baking sheet/tray in a single layer and top each with a slice of tomato, a slice of mozzarella cheese, and a sprinkling of finely chopped fresh oregano. Place under the broiler/grill for about 1 minute, just long enough to melt the cheese and heat the steak, being careful not to overcook.

RIB-EYE STEAK WITH CHIMICHURRI AND PATAGONIAN POTATOES

Many Argentine cooks keep a jar of homemade chimichurri sauce in the fridge (it keeps for several weeks) to either marinate or season cooked meats throughout the week. Chimichurri is always better after a few days, so it is often prepared on a Wednesday or Thursday to be ready for the weekend *asado* (barbecue). This recipe, from chef Francis Mallmann, pairs it with rib-eye and crunchy Patagonian potatoes. It is an Argentine classic.

CHIMICHURRI

1 cup/240 ml water

1 tbsp coarse sea salt

2 tbsp red pepper flakes

½ cup/15 g finely chopped fresh flat-leaf parsley

3 bay leaves

1 tbsp finely chopped fresh rosemary

2 tbsp finely chopped fresh thyme

1 tbsp finely chopped fresh oregano

10 garlic cloves, finely chopped

¼ cup/60 ml red wine vinegar

½ cup/120 ml extra-virgin olive oil

Six 10-oz/280-g rib-eye steaks

Coarse sea salt and freshly ground black pepper

PATAGONIAN POTATOES

3 russet potatoes

6 tsp unsalted butter

1 tsp salt

SERVES 6
as a main course

continued...

A few days before serving, make the chimichurri: In a small nonreactive saucepan, bring the water to a boil and add the salt and red pepper flakes. Remove from the heat and stir until the salt has completely dissolved. Let cool. Add the remaining ingredients and stir to combine. To store, pour into a glass jar, cover, and refrigerate for up to 1 week.

Place the steaks on a large platter and pour over ⅔ cup/165 ml of the chimichurri. Turn the steaks to coat them in the sauce. Let stand at room temperature for 2 hours.

Light a very hot fire in a large charcoal grill/barbecue or *parrilla* (Argentine grill/barbecue). Just before cooking the steaks, make the potatoes: Peel the potatoes and slice them very thinly on a mandoline or with a very sharp knife; do not place them in water as this will remove the starch and prevent the potatoes from sticking together. Divide the potatoes into 6 portions.

Heat a large cast-iron skillet over medium high heat and add 1 tsp of the butter, tilting the pan to spread the butter as it melts. In the center of the pan, lay one portion of the potatoes in a fan-like pattern, overlapping the slices. Work quickly so as not to burn the butter.

Brown the potatoes on the first side for about 4 minutes, then carefully flip them over with a metal spatula and cook for about 4 minutes on the second side. Sprinkle with a pinch of the salt, then transfer to a baking sheet/tray and keep warm in a low oven while cooking the remaining potatoes. Pour out the butter and wipe the pan with paper towels/absorbent paper. Repeat to cook the remaining potatoes, one portion at a time.

Remove the steaks from the chimichurri and season with salt and black pepper. Grill the steaks for about 6 minutes on each side for medium-rare, or until an instant-read thermometer inserted in the center of the steaks registers 135° to 140°F/57° to 60°C. Serve the steaks over the Patagonian potatoes, with a little chimichurri drizzled on top.

VENISON WITH BERRY CHUTNEY, SWEET POTATOES, AND CARAMELIZED ALMONDS

Every time I go to the Llao Llao Hotel in Bariloche, Neuquén, Patagonia, I wish I could spend more time there. The skies are bluer, the trees are greener, and the food tastes better. Rodrigo Ayala, the chef at the Llao Llao, gave me this recipe. Serve it with an old-vine smooth Pinot Noir or Malbec, so that the tannins can harmonize with the gamey sweetness of the meat and sauce.

BERRY CHUTNEY

½ pear, peeled, cored, and cut into ½-in/12-mm dice

½ apple, peeled, cored, and cut into ½-in/12-mm dice

1 red bell pepper/capsicum, seeded and cut into ½-in/12-mm dice

1 small red onion, cut into ¼-in/6-mm dice

6 tbsp/75 g brown sugar

3 tbsp apple cider vinegar

2 tbsp dried currants

2 tbsp cardamom pods, tied in a cheesecloth/muslin square

2 star anise pods

½ tsp red pepper flakes

¾ tsp salt

½ tsp freshly ground black pepper

½ cup/55 g fresh raspberries

½ cup/55 g fresh blueberries

½ cup/55 g fresh strawberries, quartered

SWEET POTATOES

2 lb/910 g orange-fleshed sweet potatoes, such as Garnet or Jewel, peeled and cut into 1-in/2.5-cm chunks

3 cups/720 ml whole milk

½ cup/100 g sugar

¾ cup/170 g (1½ sticks) unsalted butter

Pinch of salt

SERVES 6 TO 8 as a main course

CARAMELIZED ALMONDS

¼ cup/50 g sugar

1 tbsp water

¼ tsp salt

1 cup/115 g raw almonds

1½ tsp unsalted butter

One 3- to 4-lb/1.4- to 1.8-kg loin of
venison, cut into six 8-oz/225-g steaks

Salt and freshly ground black pepper

2 tbsp canola oil

½ cup/120 ml Malbec wine

1 cup/240 ml venison or chicken stock

4 tbsp/55 g cold unsalted butter, diced

Salt (optional)

For the chutney: In a large nonreactive saucepan, combine all the ingredients except the berries and cook over medium heat, stirring, until the fruits and vegetables are tender, 8 to 10 minutes. Gently stir in the berries and bring to a boil, then remove from the heat. Set aside and keep warm.

For the sweet potatoes: In a large saucepan, combine the sweet potatoes, milk, and sugar. Bring to a boil, then reduce the heat to low and simmer until the potatoes are tender, 15 to 20 minutes. Remove from the heat. Using a slotted spoon, transfer the potatoes to a food processor. Add the butter and salt and process until smooth. Return the pureed potatoes to the milk and stir until blended. Bring to a simmer, then remove from the heat. Set aside and keep warm.

For the almonds: In a medium saucepan, combine the sugar, water, and salt and stir over medium-high heat until the sugar has dissolved.

Add the almonds and butter and cook, stirring constantly, until the sugar has caramelized to a dark golden color, 4 to 6 minutes. Spread the caramelized almonds on a lightly buttered baking sheet/tray and let cool completely. Chop coarsely and set aside.

continued...

Season the venison steaks with salt and black pepper. Heat a large cast-iron frying pan over high heat. Add the oil and heat until it shimmers. Sear the venison on both sides for about 6 minutes on each side for medium-rare, or until an instant-read thermometer inserted in the center of each steak registers 130°F/55°C for medium-rare. Transfer to a platter and tent with aluminum foil.

Pour the oil out of the pan and add the wine. Cook over medium-high heat, stirring to scrape up the browned bits from the bottom of the pan. Continue to cook until reduced to about ¼ cup/60 ml. Add the stock and cook to reduce to about ¼ cup/60 ml. Remove from the heat and whisk in the cold butter a little at a time. Taste and add salt if needed.

To serve: Spoon a mound of sweet potatoes on each plate and place a venison steak next to it. Sprinkle some of the almonds on the sweet potatoes. Drizzle a spoonful of sauce over the venison, and garnish each plate with a few spoonfuls of the berry chutney.

CREPES WITH DULCE DE LECHE

Dulce de leche, a jam made of slow-cooked milk and sugar, is as much a part of the Argentine identity as gauchos and *che* (*Che* is the nickname of Argentina's revolutionary Che Guevara, as well as an expression that means "hey you," in Argentine slang). The most common daily breakfast for Argentine children is a piece of toast with butter and dulce de leche on top. Cereals and milk are virtually unheard of. In our family, *panqueques de dulce de leche*—dulce de leche crepes—were a special treat that my mother made for us on Sundays and holidays. This recipe comes from Vanina Chimeno and Francis Mallmann at Restaurante 1884 in Mendoza.

CREPES

2 large eggs

1½ cups/195 g all-purpose/plain flour

2 cups/480 ml whole milk

¼ cup/60 ml water

¼ tsp salt

1 tsp granulated sugar

4 tbsp/55 g unsalted butter, melted

6 tsp unsalted butter for greasing pan

DULCE DE LECHE

4 cups/960 ml whole milk

1¼ cups/250 g granulated sugar

½ vanilla bean/pod, split lengthwise

¼ tsp baking soda/bicarbonate of soda

Confectioners'/icing sugar for dusting

SERVES 6
as a dessert

continued...

For the crepes: In a blender, combine the eggs, flour, milk, water, salt, and sugar. Blend until smooth. With the machine running, gradually drizzle in the melted butter. Strain through a fine-mesh sieve into a bowl. Cover and refrigerate for at least 2 hours or overnight.

In an 8-in/20-cm crepe pan or frying pan, melt ½ tsp of the butter over medium-high heat. Pour about 3 tablespoons of batter into the center of the pan and tilt the pan until the batter covers the bottom of the pan. Cook for about 1 minute, then turn the crepe and cook for about 30 seconds on the second side. Transfer to a plate and repeat to make 12 crepes, stacking them as you go with sheets of parchment/baking paper between them.

For the dulce de leche: In a medium saucepan, bring the milk to a boil and add all the remaining ingredients. Reduce the heat to low and simmer, stirring frequently, until reduced to about 1½ cups/360 ml, 60 to 90 minutes. Strain into a clean jar and let cool to room temperature. To store, cover and refrigerate for up to 6 weeks. You can also buy dulce de leche at a specialty store.

Preheat the oven to 350°F/180°C/gas 4. To assemble the crepes: Place 2 tbsp dulce de leche in the center of a crepe. Fold the crepe in half, then in half again to make a triangle shape. Place on a baking sheet/tray. Repeat to fill and fold the remaining crepes, placing them on the pan in a single layer. Heat in the oven for just 2 or 3 minutes; any longer will dry out the crepes and cause the dulce de leche to run.

Place 2 crepes on each plate and dust with confectioners'/icing sugar. Serve at once.

ALFAJORES DE MAIZENA

One gift that my children and friends in San Francisco always ask me to bring back from Argentina is *alfajores*. Of Arabic origin, these are cookies sandwiched with dulce de leche in the middle. The pastry is so light in this recipe from my mother, Elena Catena, that the wafers crumble in your mouth. Alfajores can also be made with plain flour rather than corn flour. The coconut on the sides gives these alfajores a Christmas-y look and adds crunchiness.

1 cup/115 g cornstarch (cornflour)

1¾ cups/225 g all-purpose/plain flour

½ tsp baking powder

½ tsp salt

1 cup/225 g (2 sticks) unsalted butter, at room temperature

½ cup/50 g confectioners'/icing sugar

1 tbsp brandy, preferably pisco (Argentine brandy)

1 tsp vanilla extract

Dulce de Leche (page 189)

½ cup/60 g sweetened shredded coconut, toasted and finely chopped (optional); see note

MAKES 24 cookies

Position an oven rack in the center of the oven and preheat the oven to 350°F/180°C/gas 4. Line 2 baking sheets/trays with parchment/baking paper.

Sift the cornstarch/cornflour, flour, baking powder, and salt into a medium bowl. Stir with a whisk to blend. Stir in the butter with a wooden spoon, until smooth and creamy. Stir in the sugar, brandy, and vanilla until blended.

On a lightly floured board, form the dough into a 6-in/15-cm disk. Cover in plastic wrap/cling film and refrigerate for at least 30 minutes or up to 24 hours.

On a lightly floured board, roll out the dough to a $\frac{1}{4}$-in/6-mm thickness. Using a 2-in/5-cm cookie cutter, cut into rounds. Place the rounds on the prepared pans. Bake one pan of cookies at a time for 15 to 18 minutes, or until very lightly browned. Let cool for 5 minutes on the baking sheet, then carefully transfer the cookies to a wire rack to cool completely.

To assemble the cookies: Spread 1 tsp dulce de leche in an even layer on one upside-down cookie, then place another cookie right side up on top and gently press together. Roll the edges in toasted coconut, if you like.

Toasting coconut: Spread coconut on a rimmed baking sheet/tray and toast in a preheated 350°F/180°C/gas 4 oven until golden brown, 4 to 6 minutes, watching carefully to avoid burning.

HELADO DE TORRONTÉS

I believe that everyone should own an ice cream maker and that everyone should taste a Torrontés from Salta at least once in her life. This recipe, graciously given to me by Ursula Hess at the Colomé Winery, was therefore an automatic addition to the book. Argentines love ice cream, and Argentine ice cream—which is available in outdoor venues throughout the country—is as good as the best gelato that I've sampled in Italy. This one has the flowery perfume of Torrontés wine, and the creaminess and grainy texture of homemade ice cream. Be careful whom you serve it to: It is sensual, sweet, and very addictive. Serve with little cookies or fresh fruit—melon would complement the melon flavor of the Torrontés.

8 large egg yolks

2 cups/400 g sugar

2½ cups/600 ml Torrontés wine

2 cups/480 ml heavy/double cream

In a medium stainless-steel bowl, whisk together the egg yolks, sugar, and wine until blended. Place the bowl over a saucepan with 2 in/5 cm of simmering water and whisk until the mixture has thickened and doubled in volume, 10 to 12 minutes.

Remove from the heat, let cool, and cover with plastic wrap/cling film pressed directly onto the surface of the custard. Refrigerate overnight.

In a deep bowl, beat the cream to form soft peaks and fold into the chilled custard. Freeze in an ice cream maker according to the manufacturer's instructions.

QUINCE DESSERT

I simply love quince. When cooked, the bright yellow fruit turns ruby-violet—
the color of Malbec. I love the tree's beautiful flowers, and desserts made with
its fruit. Quince paste with cheese and walnuts is one of the most traditional
Argentine deserts. Because it is so hard and acidic, even when fully ripe, the
quince fruit has to be cooked to be eaten. Quince has a graininess and texture
that make it particularly delectable and different from other fruits. This recipe
for quince cooked in a sweet syrup of Malbec was given to me by Cecilia Diaz
Chuit, the owner of Cavas Wine Lodge in Mendoza, whose property is sur-
rounded by old quince trees.

3 large quince, peeled, seeded, and cut
into ½-in-/12-mm-thick slices

2 tbsp fresh lemon juice

2 cups/480 ml Malbec wine

2 cups/400 g sugar

One 3-in/7.5-cm cinnamon stick

5 cardamom pods

Vanilla ice cream or crème fraîche
for serving

SERVES 4 TO 6
as a dessert

Put the quince in a large nonreactive saucepan and add water to cover. Add
the lemon juice and bring to a boil, then reduce the heat to low and simmer for
10 minutes. Drain in a colander and set aside.

In the same saucepan, combine the wine, sugar, cinnamon, and cardamom.
Bring to a boil and cook for 5 minutes, then add the quince; the syrup should
just cover the fruit. Reduce the heat to low and simmer for 5 to 8 minutes, stirring gently from time to time, until the syrup has thickened. Remove from the
heat. Serve warm or at room temperature, with ice cream or crème fraîche.

WINE
GLOSSARY

biodynamic: Biodynamic farming is based on the concept of treating the farm or vineyard—and the plants and animals that inhabit it—as a living organism. The natural microorganisms in the soil are regenerated through composted materials with the objective of creating a balanced, self-sustaining environment. Biodynamic vineyards, where the vines are part of a living ecosystem, are farmed organically and also follow ancient folk practices, such as planting according to the phases of the moon. This method of farming is based on the ideas of the Austrian philosopher Rudolf Steiner (1861–1925).

bodega: In most of the Spanish-speaking world, *bodega* means "wine cellar" or "small grocery store." In Argentina, however, the word means "winery," and is often used in the plural, *bodegas,* in reference to the many cellaring buildings that make up a winery.

Bonarda: Until recently, when a team of UC-Davis and Argentine scientists performed DNA typing, Argentine Bonarda was thought to be a descendant of the northern Italian Bonarda. The team of scientists discovered that Argentine Bonarda is actually Corbeau (also known as Charbono, Douce Noire, and Charbonneau), a grape varietal (grape type) originally from the Savoie region of France. Unlike Malbec, which grows best in very high-altitude areas, the late-ripening Bonarda is king in El Este, eastern Mendoza, where the altitude is lower and the climate is warmer. Bonarda is generally grown in the traditional Italian pergola system where the vines create a beautiful interlacing green-leaf canopy that shields the grapes from the heat.

Criolla: A thick-skinned pink grape, cousin of the Californian Mission grape and the Chilean País. In Argentina, Criolla grapes are used to make simple white or rosé table wine. It's believed that the predecessor to Criolla was first brought to Argentina in the sixteenth century by the Spanish conquistadors and the priests who used it to make sacramental wines and liqueurs. In the sixteenth and seventeenth centuries, the vines were allowed to reproduce in the wild, giving rise to today's Criolla.

cuvée: A French word used by winemakers around the world to refer to a blend of wines from different vineyards or lots.

domaine: A term used for "wine estate" in France, generally when the wine is produced only from vineyards owned by the estate owner's winery.

grand cru: This term means "great growth" in French. It refers to historic vineyard sites in France qualified as "superior" by the AOC (appellation d'origine contrôleé) system of classification.

hang time: Refers to the number of days that the grapes stay on the vine between *véraison* (when the berries change from green to their ultimate color) and harvest. In climates where sunlight and moderate temperatures persist through early autumn, hang time can be extended. Some winemakers think that longer hang times lead to richer flavors and smoother tannins. Because sugar levels in grapes increase with time, a long hang time can result in wines that are unusually high in alcohol. In high-altitude Argentina, however, the cool climate allows for a long hang time without excessive sugar accumulation— sugars increase very slowly when the weather is cool. The resulting wines have enhanced concentration and flavors but not an excessive content of alcohol (in wine, alcohol comes from the fermentation of the sugars in the crushed grapes' juice).

maceration: During the process of fermentation, maceration occurs when the skins of the fruit are kept in contact with the juice-turned-alcohol in order to extract more flavors and tannins.

Malbec: Argentina's signature red varietal. Malbec is one of the five wine varietals (grape types) that can be used in a Bordeaux blend (the other four varietals that are authorized to be part of a Bordeaux blend are Cabernet Sauvignon, Merlot, Cabernet Franc, and Petit Verdot). Bordeaux is where the world's famous *grands crus* come from, wines such as Château Lafite, Château Latour, and Château Haut-Brion. In the eighteenth century, Malbec and Cabernet Sauvignon were the main grapes in the Medoc, where almost all of the *grands crus* are grown. Today Malbec is much more important in Argentina than in France. Malbec was brought to Argentina by Michel Aimé Pouget, a Frenchman who was commissioned by the Argentine government to start a vine nursery in Mendoza. Malbec is the most widely planted red varietal in Mendoza. It is known for its ripe cassis and black fruit aromatics and rich, smooth tannins. Malbec is a versatile grape. Depending on the region where it is grown, the age of the vines, and the soil types, it can make simple wines or dark, rich, and age-worthy wines.

minerality: A wine with minerality has flavors that have been variously described as "flinty," chalky," "like wet stones," and "earthy." Wines from cooler climates, in particular, tend to have a mineral mouthfeel; the grapes have higher acidity. Minerality is often used in reference to the white wines of Burgundy or the Loire Valley. In Argentina, minerality is found in the cooler districts within the Uco Valley, such as Gualtallary in Tupungato and Eugenio Bustos in San Carlos.

mouthfeel: The sensation on the mouth after a wine is swished and swirled. Typical descriptors of mouthfeel are *smooth, tannic, rich, soft,* and *astringent.* In general terms, wines with a large amount of tannins will taste more concentrated and astringent. The tannins that come from the skins tend to be less astringent than those that come from the seeds. Tannins from well-ripened berries that have undergone a lengthy hang-time tend to be smoother. High-acid, dry wines can often feel astringent on the palate, yet the high acid may help these wines retain their freshness and allow them to age longer. Recent research suggests that polysaccharides—molecules related to sugar that are found in grapes—may play an important role in making wines taste smooth even when they are high in tannins. Malbec is known to have a high content of polysaccharides, which may explain why Argentine Malbec can taste both rich and smooth at the same time.

négociant: The term *négociant* originates from France. *Négociants* are wine dealers who sell a range of wines, from the ultra-premium *grands crus* to blended wines that are purchased in bulk. A *"négociant* wine" generally refers to a wine in bulk that is selected by a *négociant* wine merchant and bottled under the *négociant*'s label.

nose: The aroma or bouquet of a wine. The "nose" varies from one varietal to another and from one vineyard and region to another.

old vines: Many winemakers believe that an old vine—defined as one older than twenty-five to fifty years, depending on whom you ask—is better equipped to attain a perfect balance with its soil and climate, resulting in the production of a lower yield of highly concentrated grapes.

own-rooted: Refers to *Vitis vinifera* plants, such as Cabernet Sauvignon and Chardonnay, that are grown on their own roots and not grafted onto American rootstocks.

oxidized wine/oxidative winemaking: In modern winemaking, wines are protected from excessive oxidations—contact with oxygen—so that they retain varietal character—in the nose and on the palate. When a wine is allowed to come into contact with a significant amount of oxygen during barrel aging and racking, the result is an oxidized wine. Oxidized wines quickly lose their varietal character and can even acquire aromas of sherry or Madeira (without the sweetness). Prior to the 1970s and 1980s, most Italian and Spanish wines were made in the oxidative style.

parral: A traditional raised pergola grapevine training system that is common in El Este—eastern Mendoza—and also found in the Veneto, Italy, and in Spain's northwest region. Because the *parral* pergola creates a leafy canopy that shields the berries from the intense sun, it is particularly useful in warm areas (such as eastern Mendoza). It also provides protection from frost, because the grape bunches are so high up above the soil.

phylloxera: An aphid-like insect that has been the scourge of vineyards around the world. This pest feeds on the roots and leaves of grapevines and has been responsible for the decimation of vineyards around the world, most notably during the phylloxera plague in Europe in the nineteenth century, and more recently in California in the 1980s.

protective style: A style of winemaking that minimizes oxygen exposure during aging by storing wines in stainless-steel tanks. The protective style is used to preserve varietal and individual vineyard characteristics in the aromas and flavors of a wine.

ripe style: A wine made in the ripe style is made with grapes that have been allowed to hang on the vine well into the first month of autumn. These wines tend to be higher in alcohol and to have candied and jammy flavors and aromas. In the United States, Zinfandel is often made in this style.

stainless-steel tank: Generally, a temperature-controlled tank in which grape juice is fermented and the sugars turn to alcohol. The temperature control allows for the retention of aromas and flavors.

tannins: Polyphenolic compounds in the skins and seeds of the grape cluster that are responsible for much of the character and depth of a wine. It is tannins that give red wine its texture on the mid-palate and finish. The tannin content in wine varies considerably. Heavy wines such as a Cabernet Sauvignon from a good vineyard tend to have a high concentration of tannins. More delicate wines such as Pinot Noir tend to have a lesser amount of tannins, and derive their delectability from aromatic compounds and the character, not the quantity, of their tannins.

terroir: A French term that attempts to define the effects of soil, climate, and farming practices on the taste of a wine. The French term *gout de terroir* ("taste of *terroir*") refers to the particular aromas and flavors that make a wine taste as if it could have only been grown in a specific region or vineyard. *Terroir* is the reason why a certain varietal of the same genetic stock can yield remarkably different wines depending on the place where it is grown.

tête de cuvée: The top wine of a winery.

tipicity: A wine with great "tipicity" is a wine that has the distinctive taste and aromas that are characteristic of the varietal, vineyard, and region that it comes from.

Torrontés: A white grape varietal and the only truly native Argentine varietal. Torrontés smells like an ultra-ripe Riesling and tastes like a slightly sweeter version of Pinot Grigio. The best Torrontés comes from Salta, a province in the northernmost part of Argentina.

ungrafted: Same as own-rooted.

varietal: A grape "type," such as Cabernet Sauvignon, Chardonnay, or Malbec, that has a specific genetic makeup, leaf shape, and flavor profile.

vinify: To make wine from the juice of a grapevine through the process of fermentation.

BIBLIOGRAPHY

Archetti, Eduardo P. *Masculinities: Football, Polo, and the Tango in Argentina.* Oxford, U.K.: Berg, 1999. *The Journal of the Royal Anthropological Institute* called this book a "fascinating introduction to the worlds of male-dominated sports in Argentina, and how notions of maleness are related to the formation of a national identity."

Borges, Jorge Luis. *Collected Fictions.* New York: Penguin, 1999. The Argentine writer and poet Jorge Luis Borges (1899–1986) has been called one of the twentieth century's most influential writers, particularly in the short-story genre. Every one of his short stories appears here for the first time in one volume, translated and annotated by University of Puerto Rico professor Andrew Hurley.

——— *Labyrinths: Selected Stories & Other Writings.* New York: New Directions, 2007. David Foster Wallace wrote of Borges: "[He] is arguably the great bridge between modernism and postmodernism in world literature." This English-language collection of Borges's works contains the author's most notable short stories and essays.

Bracken, James. *Che Boludo! A Gringo's Guide to Understanding the Argentines.* Bariloche: Editorial Caleuche, 2008. A gringo's guide to understanding the Argentines through their slang.

Foster, David William, Melissa Fitch Lockhart, and Darrell B. Lockhart. *Culture and Customs of Argentina.* Westport, CT: Greenwood Press, 1998. *Library Journal* called this collection of works on Argentina's customs " . . . an excellent historical and contemporary overview of Argentina's rich cultural tradition."

Gargiulo, Julieta and Agustín Borzi. *Il Vino si fa così* ("This Is How Wine Is Made"). Buenos Aires: Polo Rossi Casa Editorial, 2004. Julieta Gargiulo, Mendozan cultural ambassador, and Agustín Borzi, Mendozan winemaker and historian, trace the history of Mendoza's wine industry back to the nineteenth century. The book focuses on the contribution of Italian immigrants to Argentine wine, and on the fluid exchange of ideas and know-how between the immigrants and their Italian homeland. Note that the title is Italian, but the book is in Spanish.

Goldin, Carlos. *The Secrets of Argentine Malbec.* Buenos Aires: Focus, 2004. During the 2002 grape harvest in Mendoza, Argentine photographer Carlos Goldin traveled to Argentina's wine country to cover the nation's signature wine, Malbec, and the result is this sumptuous full-color coffee-table book on Argentine Malbec. In Goldin's own words: "I traveled through our country's winemaking zones. I visited dozens of wineries, I walked through the rows of vines, I was entranced by the one-of-a-kind scent of flowering grapevines. I tasted Argentina's best Malbec wines, I learned a tremendous amount. The secrets of this fascinating wine were gradually revealed to me."

Mallmann, Francis and Peter Kaminsky. *Seven Fires: Grilling the Argentine Way.* New York: Artisan, 2009. *The New York Times* writes: "[Mallman] reconnects us to the primal simplicity and visceral pleasure of cooking over fire."

Nouzeilles, Gabriela and Graciela Montaldo, eds. *The Argentina Reader.* Durham, NC: Duke University Press, 2003. This rich and fascinating compilation has been called "the best introduction for English readers to [Argentina's] history, culture, and society . . . [and] subtly conveys the admirable and loathsome qualities of a complicated and in many ways unfathomable society" (Benjamin Schwarz, *The Atlantic Monthly*).

Rolland, Michel and Enrique Chrabolowsky. *Wines of Argentina.* Buenos Aires: Mirrol, 2003. Now in its third edition, this instant classic has beautiful photographs and an impeccable pedigree: The text was written by famed winemaker Michel Rolland and wine journalist Enrique Chrabolowsky. Three hundred Argentine wineries, one per page, are featured with photos, historical information, and wine recommendations.

Romero, Luis Alberto. *A History of Argentina in the Twentieth Century.* University Park: Penn State Press, 2002. A professor of history at the Universidad de Buenos Aires in Argentina, Romero is the son of one of Argentina's greatest twentieth-century historians, José Luis Romero. This work has been described as "an excellent history, with a fine balance between the economic, the political and the social. Romero is particularly good on the social history of the earlier twentieth century, charting the effects of the rapid cultural modernization that would be created by Peronism's promise of welfare and cultural autarky" (Jon Beasley-Murray, *Times Literary Supplement*).

Sarmiento, Domingo Faustino. *Facundo, or Civilization and Barbarism.* Berkeley: University of California Press, 2003. This classic work, a cornerstone of Latin American literature, was written in 1845 by Domingo Faustino

Sarmiento as a clarion call to progress for a burgeoning nation. An educator and writer, Sarmiento was president of Argentina from 1868 to 1874.

———. *Recollections of a Provincial Past*. New York: Oxford University Press, 2005. This is perhaps the best-known of Sarmiento's several autobiographies. "*Recollections of a Provincial Past* is one of the indisputable classics of Spanish-American literature, as well as one of the earliest autobiographies written in the Americas in Spanish. Written in exile in 1850, the memoirs describe his childhood and adolescence in the Andean province of San Juan whose customs were still those of a colony. Sarmiento presents his life as the triumph of civilization over barbarism; looking back on his youth, he measures his wealth and strength by the accumulation of enriching personal and political experiences" (Oxford University Press).

Scobie, James R. *Argentina: A City and a Nation*. New York: Oxford University Press, 1964. The late historian James Scobie spent many years living, researching, and writing about the Latin American experience. He was an expert on Argentina, and the author of a substantial body of scholarly books and articles in the field of Latin American urban history. This historical work encompasses not only politics and economics but also literature and art.

———. *Secondary Cities of Argentina: The Social History of Corrientes, Salta, and Mendoza, 1850–1910*. Palo Alto, CA: Stanford University Press, 1988. This book delves into how demographics and social factors affect a region's economic growth. In a review, Jeremy Adelman called this book "a gem. The late James Scobie's previous books have become classics and continue to be basic reading for students of Latin American history decades after their publication. *Secondary Cities of Argentina* will no doubt enjoy the same fate."

Shumway, Nicholas. *The Invention of Argentina*. Berkeley: University of California Press, 1993. This classic cultural history details the country's efforts to determine its nature, its destiny, and its place among the nations of the world.

Slatta, Richard W. *Gauchos & the Vanishing Frontier*. Lincoln: University of Nebraska Press, 1992. The history of this nineteenth-century migratory ranch hand is told in fascinating detail by Richard W. Slatta, a professor of history at North Carolina State University at Raleigh.

Phone numbers are listed with the provincial code in parentheses followed by the local number. If you are calling from abroad, you will need to add the country code for Argentina, which is 54. If you are calling from one province to another (e.g., from Buenos Aires to Mendoza) you will need to add 0 before the provincial code.

Here is an example of how you would call 1884 Restaurant in Mendoza from various locations:

FROM US: 01154 261 424 2682

FROM UK: 0054 261 424 2682

FROM AN INTERNATIONAL CELL PHONE: +54 261 424 2682

FROM BUENOS AIRES: 0261 424 2682

A few of the street addresses are followed by the denomination s/n, which means *sin nombre,* without a name, indicating that there is no specific street number for the winery location. Some numbers provided are international cell phone numbers.

Winery hours are variable, so always call ahead for reservations before visiting. Bars and restaurants open "until close" generally shut down between 2 A.M. and 4 A.M.

Chapter Three: Mendoza City

1884 – Restaurant
Address: Belgrano 1188, Godoy Cruz
Phone: 261 424 2698
Web site: www.1884restaurante.com.ar
Open days and hours: Daily 8:30 P.M.–12 A.M.
Reservations required: Yes

Azafrán – Restaurant
Address: Av. Sarmiento 765, Downtown Mendoza
Phone: 261 429 4200
Web site: www.bve.com.ar
Open days and hours: Daily 12 P.M.–1 A.M.
Reservations required: Recommended

Bistro M (Park Hyatt) – Restaurant
Address: Chile 1124, Downtown Mendoza
Phone: 261 441 1200
Web site: www.mendoza.park.hyatt.com
Open days and hours: Breakfast: Daily 6:30–11 A.M.; Lunch: Daily 12:30–3:30 P.M.; Dinner: Sun–Wed 8:30 P.M.–12 A.M., Thu–Sat 8:30 P.M.–1 A.M.
Reservations required: Recommended

Bodegas CARO – Winery
Address: Pte Alvear 151, Godoy Cruz
Phone: 261 424 6477
Web site: www.bodegascaro.com
Open days and hours: By appointment only

Don Mario – Restaurant
Address: 25 de Mayo 1324, Dorrego, Guaymallén
Phone: 261 431 0810
Web site: www.donmario.com.ar
Open days and hours: Daily 12:30–4 P.M. and 8 P.M.–12:30 A.M.
Reservations required: No

Escorihuela Gascón – Winery
Address: Belgrano 1188, Godoy Cruz
Phone: 261 424 2282
Web site: www.escorihuelagascon.com.ar
Open days and hours: Mon–Fri 10 A.M.–1 P.M. and 2:30 P.M.–5 P.M.
Reservations required: Recommended

Francesco Ristorante
Address: Chile 1268, Downtown Mendoza
Phone: 261 429 7182
Web site: www.francescoristorante.com.ar
Open days and hours: Mon–Sat 7 P.M.–1 A.M.
Reservations required: Recommended

La Barra – Restaurant
Address: Av. Belgrano 1086, Downtown
Mendoza
Phone: 261 15 654 1950
Open days and hours: Mon–Fri 8–11 P.M.
Reservations required: Yes. Cash only

Park Hyatt Mendoza – Hotel
Address: Chile 1124, Downtown Mendoza
Phone: 261 441 1234
Web site: www.mendoza.park.hyatt.com

The Vines of Mendoza Tasting Room
Address: Espejo 567, Downtown Mendoza
Phone: 261 438 1031
Web site: www.vinesofmendoza.com
Open days and hours: Mon–Sat 3–10 P.M.

Chapter Four:
El Este: Eastern Mendoza

Casa Argento – Winery Tasting Rooms
Address: Justicia 28, Chacras de Coria
Phone: 261 496 3699
Web site: www.argentowine.com

Familia Zuccardi – Winery
Address: Ruta Provincial N 33 Km 7,5,
Fray Luis Beltrán, Maipú
Phone: 261 441 0000
Web site: www.familiazuccardi.com
Open days and hours: Mon–Sat 9 A.M.–5 P.M.;
Sun and holidays 10 A.M.–4 P.M.
Reservations required: No

Chapter Five: Primera Zona:
Maipú and Northern Luján de Cuyo

Almacén del Sur – Restaurant
Address: Sanichelli 709, Coquimbito, Maipú
Phone: 261 410 6597
Web site: www.almacendelsur.com
Open days and hours: Lunch only: Mon–Sat
Reservations required: Yes

Alta Vista – Winery
Address: Álzaga 3972 , Chacras de Coria,
Luján de Cuyo
Phone: 261 496 4684
Web site: www.altavistawines.com
Open days and hours: Daily 9 A.M.–6 P.M.
Reservations required: Yes

Altos las Hormigas – Winery
Address: Calle La Legua s/n, Medrano
Phone: 261 424 3727
Web site: www.altolashormigas.com

Bodega Benegas – Winery
Address: Carril Araoz al 1600, Mayor
Drummond, Luján de Cuyo
Phone: 261 496 0794
Web site: www.bodegabenegas.com
Open days and hours: Call to inquire

Bodegas López
Address: Ozamis 375, Maipú
Phone: 261 497 2406
Web site: www.bodegaslopez.com
Open days and hours: Mon–Fri, 9 A.M.–5 P.M.;
Saturdays until noon
Reservations required: Yes; must arrive on the
hour for a tour

Bodega Vistalba – Winery
Address: R. Saenz Peña 3531, Vistalba,
Luján de Cuyo
Phone: 261 498 2330
Web site: www.carlospulentawines.com
Open days and hours: Mon–Fri
Reservations required: Yes, 24 hrs. in advance

Bodegas y Viñedos Pascual Toso
Address: Alberdi 808, San José, Guaymallen
Phone: 261 405 8000
Web site: www.bodegastoso.com.ar

**Cap Vistalba – Winery, Lodge, and
La Bourgogne Restaurant**
Address: Roque Saenz Peña 3531, Visalba
Phone: 261 498 9400
Web site: www.carlospulentawines.com

Casa Argento – Winery tasting room
Address: Justicia 28, Chacras de Coria
Phone: 261 496 3699
Web site: www.argentowine.com

Club Tapiz – Restaurant and Lodge
Address: Pedro Molina 5517, Maipú
Phone: 261 496 4815
Web site: www.tapiz.com

Enrique Foster – Winery
Address: San Martin 5039, Carrodilla,
Luján de Cuyo.
Phone: +54 261 496 1579
Web site: www.enriquefoster.com

Fabre Montmayou – Winery
Address: Roque Saenz Peña s/n, Vistalba
Phone: 261 498 2330
Web site: www.domainevistalba.com
Open days and hours: Mon–Fri
Reservations required: Yes, 24 hrs. in advance

La Bourgogne – Restaurant
Address: R. Saenz Peña 3531, Vistalba
Phone: 261 498 9400
Web site: www.carlospulentawines.com
Open days and hours: Lunch only: Tue–Sat
Reservations required: Yes

La Rural Wine Museum – Winery
Address: Montecaseros 2625, Coquimbito,
Maipú
Phone: 261 497 2013
Web site: www.larural.com
Open days and hours: Mon–Sat 9 A.M.–1 P.M.
and 2 P.M.–5 P.M.
Reservations required: Yes

Lagarde – Winery
Address: San Martin 1745, Mayor Drummond,
Luján de Cuyo
Phone: 261 498 0011
Web site: www.lagarde.com.ar
Open days and hours: Mon–Fri
9:30 A.M.–5:30 P.M.
Reservations required: Yes

Luigi Bosca – Winery
Address: San Martin 2044, Mayor
Drummond, Luján de Cuyo
Phone: 261 498 1974
Web site: www.luigibosca.com.ar
Open days and hours: Mon–Fri 10 A.M.;
Sat 11 A.M.
Reservations required: Yes

Mendel – Winery
Address: Terrada 1863, Mayor Drummond,
Luján de Cuyo
Phone: 261 524 1621
Web site: www.mendel.com.ar
Open days and hours: Mon–Fri
9:30 A.M.–1 P.M.
Reservations required: Yes

Nieto Senetiner – Winery
Address: Guardia Vieja s/n, Vistalba,
Luján de Cuyo
Phone: 261 498 0315
Web site: www.nietosenetiner.com.ar
Open days and hours: Daily 10 A.M.–3 P.M.
Reservations required: Recommended

Trapiche – Winery
Address: Nueva Mayorga s/n, Coquimbito,
Maipú
Phone: 261 520 7666
Web site: www.trapiche.com.ar
Open days and hours: Mon–Fri 9 A.M.–5 P.M.;
Sat 9 A.M.–1 P.M.
Reservations required: Recommended

Trivento – Winery
Address: Canal Pescara 9347, Russell, Maipú
Phone: 261 413 7100
Web site: www.trivento.com
Open days and hours: Call to inquire

Chapter Six:
Luján de Cuyo: Perdriel

Achaval-Ferrer – Winery
Address: Cobos 2601, Perdriel, Luján de Cuyo
Phone: 261 400 1131
Web site: www.achaval-ferrer.com
Open days and hours: Daily 9 A.M.–3 P.M.
Reservations required: Yes

Bodegas Renacer – Winery
Address: Brandsen 1863, Perdriel,
Luján de Cuyo
Phone: 261 524 4416
Web site: www.bodegarenacer.com.ar
Open days and hours: Mon–Fri 9 A.M.–6 P.M.
Reservations required: Yes

Cavas Wine Lodge
Address: Costaflores s/n, Alto Agrelo
Phone: 261 410 6927
Web site: www.cavaswinelodge.com

Melipal – Winery
Address: Ruta 7 Km 1056, Agrelo,
Luján de Cuyo
Phone: 261 524 8040
Web site: www.bodegamelipal.com
Open days and hours: Mon–Fri 11 A.M.;
Sat 11:30 A.M.
Reservations required: Yes

Norton – Winery
Address: Ruta 15 Km 23,5, Perdriel,
Luján de Cuyo
Phone: 261 490 9700
Web site: www.norton.com.ar

Open days and hours: Mon–Sat
9 A.M.–4:30 P.M.
Reservations required: Yes

Ruca Malen – Winery
Address: Ruta Nacional 7 Km 1059, Agrelo,
Luján de Cuyo
Phone: 261 562 8357
Web site: www.bodegarucamalen.com
Open days and hours: Mon–Fri 10 A.M.–4 P.M.;
Sat 10 A.M. and 11 A.M.
Tour with lunch: Daily 12 P.M.–3 P.M.
Reservations required: Yes

Terrazas de Los Andes – Winery
Address: Thames y Cochabamba, Perdriel,
Luján de Cuyo
Phone: 261 488 0058
Web site: www.terrazasdelosandes.com
Open days and hours: Mon–Fri 10 A.M.
Reservations required: Yes

Viña Cobos – Winery
Address: Costa Flores y Ruta 7, Perdriel,
Luján de Cuyo
Phone: 261 479 0130
Web site: www.vinacobos.com
Open days and hours: Mon–Fri 12 P.M.
Reservations required: Yes

Chapter Seven: Luján de Cuyo: Agrelo and Ugarteche

Belasco de Baquedano – Winery
Address: Cobos 8260, Agrelo, Luján de Cuyo
Phone: 261 524 7864
Web site: www.familiabelasco.com
Open days and hours: Daily 10 A.M.–4 P.M.
Reservations required: Recommended

Bodega Catena Zapata – Winery
Address: Cobos s/n, Agrelo, Luján de Cuyo
Phone: 261 413 1124
Web site: www.catenazapata.com
Open days and hours: Mon–Fri 9:30 A.M.–3:30 P.M.; Sat 9:30 and 11 A.M.
Reservations required: Yes

Cavas Wine Lodge – Boutique Hotel and Restaurant
Address: Costaflores s/n, Agrelo, Luján de Cuyo
Phone: 261 410 6927
Web site: www.cavaswinelodge.com
Open days and hours: Restaurant open daily for lunch and dinner at 11:30 A.M. and 7:30 P.M.
Reservations required: Yes

Dolium – Winery
Address: Ruta Provincial 15 Km 30 s/n, Agrelo, Luján de Cuyo
Phone: 261 490 0190
Web site: www.dolium.com
Open days and hours: Mon–Fri 10 A.M.–4:30 P.M.
Reservations required: Yes

Dominio del Plata – Winery
Address: Cochabamba 7801, Agrelo, Luján de Cuyo
Phone: 261 498 9200
Web site: www.dominiodelplata.com.ar
Open days and hours: Mon–Fri 9 A.M.–5:30 P.M.
Reservations required: Yes

Doña Paula – Winery
Address: Poliducto s/n, Ugarteche, Luján de Cuyo
Web site: www.donapaula.com.ar

Finca La Anita – Winery
Address: Calle Cobos s/n, Agrelo, Luján de Cuyo
Phone: 261 490 0255
Web site: www.fincalaanita.com

Pulenta Estate – Winery
Address: Ruta Provincial 36 Km 6,5, Agrelo, Luján de Cuyo
Phone: 261 420 0800
Web site: www.pulentaestate.com
Open days and hours: Mon–Fri 9:30 A.M–4 P.M.; Sat morning only
Reservations required: Yes

Septima – Winery
Address: Ruta Internacional 7, Km 6,5, Agrelo
Phone: 261 498 5164
Web site: www.bodegaseptima.com
Open days and hours: Mon–Fri 10 A.M.–5 P.M.; Sat 10 A.M.–12 P.M.
Reservations required: Yes

Tapiz – Winery
Address: Ruta 89 Km 32, Agrelo
Phone: 261 490 0202
Web site: www.tapiz.com.ar
Open days and hours: Mon–Fri 10 A.M.–4 P.M.
Reservations required: Yes

Chapter Eight:
The Uco Valley: Tupungato

Andeluna – Winery
Address: Ruta 89 s/n, Tupungato
Phone: 262 242 3226
Web site: www.andeluna.com
Open days and hours: Daily 9 A.M.–4 P.M.
Reservations required: Yes

El Ilo – Restaurant
Address: Belgrano 703, Tupungato
Phone: 261 262 2488

Finca Sophenia – Winery
Address: Ruta 89 Km 13.5, Tupungato
Phone: 262 248 9680
Web site: www.sophenia.com.ar

Ilo Restaurant Tupungato
Address: Belgrano 703, Tupungato
Phone: 262 248 8323
Open days and hours: Lunch: Daily
11:45 A.M.–3 P.M.; Dinner: Wed–Sun
9 P.M.–12:30 A.M.
Reservations required: On weekends

Salentein – Winery
Address: Ruta 89 s/n, Esquina Elías Videla,
Los Arboles, Tupungato
Phone: 262 242 9500
Web site: www.bodegasalentein.com
Open days and hours: Sun–Mon and holidays;
guided tours 10 A.M.–4 P.M.

Salentein Posada – Bed and Breakfast
Address: Ruta 89 s/n, Tupungato
Phone: 262 242 9090
Web site: www.bodegasalentein.com
Open days and hours: Restaurant open daily
for lunch
Reservations required: Yes

Chapter Nine: The Southern Uco
Valley: Tunuyán and San Carlos

Almacén de Uco – Restaurant
Address: Ruta 89 s/n, Mazano Historico,
Tunuyán
Phone: 262 242 2134
Web site: www.almacendeuco.com
Open days and hours: Sat–Sun 12–4 P.M.
Reservations required: Yes

Altocedro – Winery
Address: Ejercito de los Andes esq. Tregea 1,
La Consulta, San Carlos
Phone: 261 423 3314
Web site: www.altocedro.com.ar

Casa Antucura – Hotel
Address: Barrandica s/n, Vistalores, Tunuyán
Phone: 261 524 8283
Web site: www.casaantucura.com

Clos de los Siete/Monteviejo – Wineries
Address: Calle Clodomiro Silva s/n,
Vista Flores, Tunuyán
Phone: 262 242 2054
Web site: www.monteviejo.com
Open days and hours: Visits arranged by
phone call with 2 days' advance notice
Reservations required: Yes

El Cielo – Restaurant
Address: San Martín y Balmaceda,
La Consulta
Phone: 262 247 0814
Open days and hours: Daily 10 A.M.–4 P.M.,
7:30 P.M.–1 A.M.
Reservations required: No

Ernesto Catena – Winery
Tikal Vineyard and Almanegra (Nakbé)
Sparkling Winery
Address: Ruta 92, Vista Flores

Phone: 11 4331 1251
Web site: www.tikalwines.com
Open days and hours: Call to inquire
Reservations required: Yes

François Lurton – Winery
Address: Ruta Provincial 94 Km 21,
Vista Flores, Tunuyán
Phone: 262 249 2078
Web site: www.jflurton.com
Open days and hours: Mon–Fri 10 A.M.–5 P.M.
Reservations required: Yes, 2 days in advance

La Posada del Jamón – Restaurant
Address: Ruta 92 Km 14, Vista Flores,
Tunuyán
Phone: 262 249 2053
Web site: www.laposadadeljamon.com.ar
Open days and hours: Daily 12 P.M.–4 P.M.
Reservations required: Recommended

O. Fournier – Winery
Address: Los Indios s/n, La Consulta,
San Carlos
Phone: 262 245 1579
Web site: www.ofournier.com
Open days and hours: Call to inquire
Reservations required: Yes

Chapter Ten: Patagonia: Río Negro and Neuquén Provinces

Bodega del Fin del Mundo – Winery
Address: Ruta Provincial 8 Km 9, San Patricio
del Chañar, Neuquén
Phone: 299 485 5004
Web site: www.bodegadelfindelmundo.com
Open days and hours: Tue–Fri 10 A.M.–4 P.M.;
Sat and holidays 10 A.M.–5 P.M.
Reservations required: Recommended

Chacra – Winery
Río Negro
Web site: www.bodegachacra.com

Familia Schroeder – Winery
Address: Calle 7 Norte, San Patricio del
Chañar, Neuquén
Phone: 9 299 489 9600
Web site: www.familiaschroeder.com.ar
Open days and hours: Mon–Fri 9 A.M.–5 P.M.;
Sat–Sun and holidays 10:30 A.M.–5:30 P.M.
Reservations required: Recommended

Humberto Canale – Winery
Address: Chacra 186, General Roca, Río Negro
Phone: 294 143 0415
Web site: www.bodegahcanale.com
Open days and hours: Thu and Fri 10:30 A.M.
Reservations required: Yes
Tasting: Yes

Llao Llao Hotel
Address: Av. Ezequiel Bustillo Km 25,
Bariloche, Neuquén
Phone: 294 444 8530
Web site: www.llaollao.com

Noemia Winery – Winery
Address: Ruta Provincial 7 Km 12, Valle Azul,
Río Negro
Phone: 294 115 530 412
Web site: www.bodeganoemia.com

NQN – Winery
Address: Ruta Provincial 7 Picada 15,
San Patricio del Chañar, Neuquén
Phone: 299 489 7500
Web site: www.bodeganqn.com
Open days and hours: Mon–Fri 9 A.M.–5 P.M.;
Sat–Sun and holidays 10:30 A.M.–4:30 P.M.
Reservations required: Recommended

Chapter Eleven: Salta

Bodega Jose L. Mounier – Finca las Nubes – Winery
Address: El Divisadero, Alto Valle de Cafayate
Phone: 3868 422 129
Web site: www.bodegamounier.com
Open days and hours: Jan–Feb 9:30 A.M.–1 P.M. and 4:30 P.M.–7 P.M.; Mar–Dec 9:30 A.M.–5 P.M.
Reservations required: Recommended

Colomé – Winery, Hotel, and Gallery
Address: Ruta Provincial 53 Km 20, Molinos
Phone: 3868 494 056
Web site: www.bodegacolome.com
Open days and hours: Daily 10 A.M. and 3 P.M.
Reservations required: Yes

El Esteco – Winery
Address: Ruta 40 y Ruta 68, Cafayate
Phone: 3868 421 139
Web site: www.elesteco.com.ar
Open days and hours: Daily 10 A.M.–12 P.M.; 2:30 P.M.–5:30 P.M.
Reservations required: Recommended

Etchart – Winery
Address: Ruta 40, Cafayate
Phone: 3868 421 310
Web site: www.bodegasetchart.com
Open days and hours: Call to inquire
Reservations required: Yes

Felix Lavaque – Finca el Recreo – Winery
Address: Ruta 40/km 4340, Cafayate
Phone: 3868 421 709
Web site: www.felixlavaque.com; www.fincaquara.com

Patios de Cafayate – Hotel
Address: Ruta Nacional 40 y Ruta Nacional 68, Cafayate
Phone: 3868 422 229

Web site: www.starwoodhotels.com
Reservations required: Yes

San Pedro de Yacochuya – Winery
Address: Ruta Provincial N 2 Km 6, Cafayate
Phone: 3868 421 233
Web site: www.sanpedrodeyacochuya.com.ar
Open days and hours: Mon–Fri 10 A.M.–6 P.M.; Sat 10 A.M.–1 P.M.
Reservations required: Yes

Chapter Twelve: Touring Buenos Aires

Astrid y Gaston – Restaurant
Address: Lafinur 3222, Palermo
Phone: 11 4802 2991
Open days and hours: Mon–Sat lunch 12:30 P.M.–3 P.M. and dinner 8:30 P.M.–11:30 P.M.
Reservations required: Recommended

Bar 878
Address: Thames 878, Villa Crespo
Phone: 11 4773 1098
Open days and hours: Mon–Fri 7 P.M.–close; Sat–Sun 8 P.M.–close

Bereber – Restaurant
Address: Armenia 1880, Palermo Soho
Phone: 11 4833 5662
Open days and hours: Daily dinner 8:30 P.M.–close; Sat–Sun lunch
Reservations required: Yes

Cabaña Las Lilas – Restaurant
Address: Av. Alicia Moreau de Justo 516, Puerto Madero
Phone: 11 4313 1336
Web site: www.laslilas.com
Open days and hours: Daily 12 P.M.– 12:30 A.M.; Fri–Sat 12 P.M.–1 A.M.
Reservations required: Recommended

Café Tortoni
Address: Av. de Mayo 825, Downtown
Phone: 11 4342 4328
Web site: www.cafetortoni.com.ar
Open days and hours: Daily 8:30 A.M.– 2 A.M.

Casa Cruz – Restaurant
Address: Uriarte 1658, Palermo Viejo
Phone: 11 4833 1112
Web site: www.casacruz-restaurant.com
Open days and hours: Mon–Sat
8:30 P.M.–closing
Reservations required: Recommended

Congo Bar
Address: Honduras 5329, Palermo Viejo
Phone: 11 4833 5857
Open days and hours: Wed–Sat 8 P.M.–3:30 A.M.

El Green Bamboo – Restaurant
Address: Costa Rica 5802, Palermo
Hollywood
Phone: 11 4775 7050
Web site: www.green-bamboo.com.ar
Open days and hours: Daily 8:30 P.M.–closing
Reservations required: Recommended

Faena Hotel – Restaurant/Bar
Address: Martha Salotti 445, Puerto Madero
Phone: 11 4010 9000
Web site: www.faenahotelanduniverse.com

Gran Bar Danzon
Address: Libertad 1161, Recoleta
Phone: 11 4811 1108
Web site: www.granbardanzon.com.ar
Open days and hours: Mon–Fri 7 A.M.–closing;
Sat and Sun 8 P.M.–closing
Reservations required: Recommended

Il Matterello – Restaurant
Address: Martin Rodríguez 517, La Boca
Phone: 11 4307 0529
Web site: www.ilmatterelloristorante.com
Open days and hours: Tue–Sun lunch and
dinner 12:30 P.M.–3 P.M. and 8:30 P.M.–12 A.M.
Reservations required: Recommended

La Bourgogne – Restaurant
Address: Ayacucho 2027, Recoleta
Phone: 11 4808 2100
Web site: www.alvearpalace.com
Open days and hours: Mon–Fri lunch
12 P.M.–4 P.M. and dinner 7:30 P.M.–12 A.M.;
Sat dinner only
Reservations required: Yes

La Brigada – Restaurant
Address: Estados Unidos 465, San Telmo
Phone: 11 4361 5557
Web site: www.labrigada.com
Open days and hours: Daily 12–3 P.M. and
8 P.M.–12 A.M.
Reservations required: Recommended

La Caballeriza – Restaurant
Address: Boulevard Chenaut, 1878,
Las Cañitas
Phone: 11 4 773 4035
Web site: www.lacaballeriza-argentina.com
Open days and hours: Daily 12–3 P.M. and
8 P.M.–12:30 A.M.
Reservations required: Recommended

La Cabaña – Restaurant
Address: Rodríguez Peña 1967, Recoleta
Phone: 11 4814 0001
Web site: www.lacabanabuenosaires.com.ar
Open days and hours: Mon–Sat 12 P.M.–12 A.M.
Reservations required: Recommended

La Cabrera – Restaurant
Address: Cabrera 5099, Palermo Soho
Phone: 11 4831 7002
Web site: www.parrillalacabrera.com.ar
Open days and hours: Tue–Sun 11 A.M.–close
Reservations required: Yes

La Dorita – Restaurant
Address: Humboldt 1911, Palermo
Phone: 11 4773 0070
Open days and hours: Daily 12 P.M.–3 P.M. and
8 P.M.–12 A.M.
Reservations required: Recommended

La Viruta – Tango classes and show
Address: Armenia 1366, Palermo
Phone: 11 4774 6357
Web site: www.lavirutatango.com.ar
Reservations required: Recommended

Libelula – Restaurant
Address: Jeronimo Salguero 2983, Palermo
Hollywood
Phone: 11 4802 7220
Web site: www.libelularestaurant.com.ar
Open days and hours: Daily 8 P.M.–2 A.M.
Reservations required: Recommended

Minga – Restaurant
Address: Costa Rica 4528, Palermo Soho
Phone: 11 4833 5775
Web site: www.mingaparrilla.com.ar
Open days and hours: Daily 9 A.M.–12:30 A.M.;
until 1:30 A.M. on weekends

Osaka – Restaurant
Address: Soler 5608, Palermo Hollywood
Phone: 11 4775 6964
Web site: www.osaka.com.pe
Open days and hours: Mon–Sat lunch
12:30P.M.–3:45 P.M. and dinner 8 P.M.–12 A.M.;
Reservations required: Yes

Oviedo – Restaurant
Address: Beruti 2602, Barrio Norte
Phone: 11 4821 3741
Web site: www.oviedoresto.com.ar
Open days and hours: Mon–Sat 12 P.M.–12 A.M.
Reservations required: Recommended

Pacha – Night Club
Address: Rafael Obligado 6151, Costanera
Phone: 11 4788 4280
Web site: www.pachabuenosaires.com
Open days and hours: Fri–Sat 12 A.M.–close

Park Hyatt Palacio Duhau – Hotel
Address: Avenida Alvear 1661, Buenos Aires
Phone: 11 5171 1234
Web site: www.buenosaires.park.hyatt.com

Patagonia Sur – Restaurant
Address: Rocha 801 esq. Pedro de Mendoza,
La Boca
Phone: 11 4303 5917
Web site: www.restaurantepatagoniasur.com
Open days and hours: Tue–Sat 12:30 P.M.–3 P.M.
and 8 P.M.–12 A.M.
Reservations required: Yes

**Plaza Grill at the Marriott Plaza Hotel –
Restaurant**
Address: Florida 1005, Downtown
Phone: 11 4318 3074
Web site: www.mariott.com
Open days and hours: Daily 12 P.M.–4 P.M. and
7 P.M.–12 A.M.

Señor Tango – Tango Show
Address: Hipolito Vieytes 1655, Barracas
Phone: 11 4303 0231
Web site: www.senortango.com.ar
Open days and hours: Daily show 9:30 P.M.
Reservations required: Yes

Sucre – Restaurant
Address: Sucre 676, Belgrano
Phone: 11 4782 9082
Web site: www.sucrerestaurant.com.ar
Open days and hours: Daily 12 P.M.–3 P.M. and
8 P.M.–12 A.M.
Reservations required: Recommended

Tegui – Restaurant
Address: Costa Rica 5852, Palermo Hollywood
Phone: 11 5291 3333
Web site: www.tegui.com.ar
Open days and hours: Tue–Sat
12:30 P.M.–3:30 P.M. and 8:30 P.M.–close
Reservations required: Yes

Tomo I – Restaurant
Address: Carlos Pellegrini 521, Downtown
Phone: 11 4326 6695
Web site: www.tomo1.com.ar
Open days and hours: Mon–Sat
7:30 P.M.–12:30 A.M.
Reservations required: Recommended

MAPS

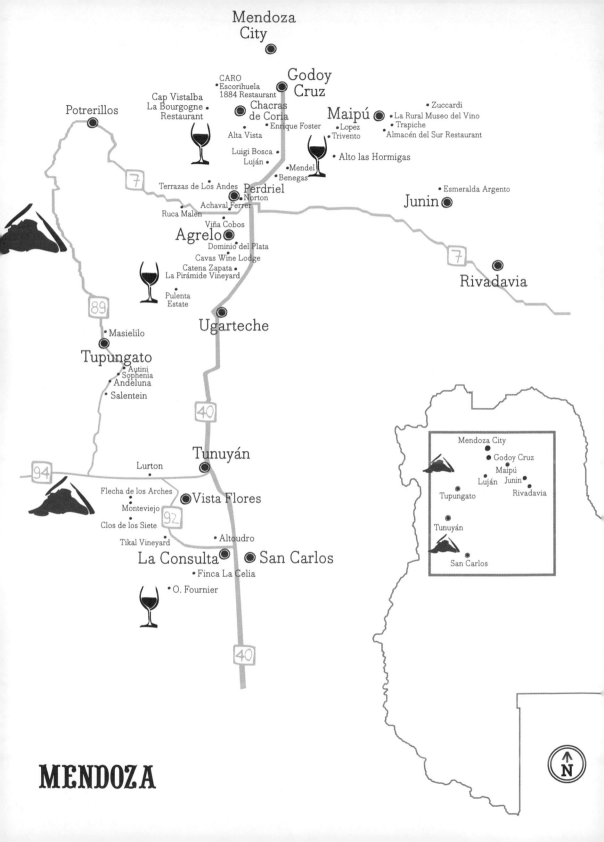

Mendoza
City

CARO
• Escorihuela   Godoy
1884 Restaurant   Cruz
Cap Vistalba
La Bourgogne   Chacras   Maipú   • Zuccardi
Restaurant   de Coria   • La Rural Museo del Vino
                • Enrique Foster   • Trapiche
        Alta Vista   • Lopez   • Almacén del Sur Restaurant
                            • Trivento
    Luigi Bosca
        Luján •   • Alto las Hormigas
                    • Mendel
                • Benegas
Potrerillos   • Esmeralda Argento
    Terrazas de Los Andes   Junin
                Perdriel
        Achaval Ferrer • Norton
    Ruca Malen •
        • Viña Cobos   7
    Agrelo •
        • Dominio del Plata   Rivadavia
        • Cavas Wine Lodge
        Catena Zapata •
        La Pirámide Vineyard •
            • Pulenta
            Estate
    89
        • Masielilo
                Ugarteche
    Tupungato
        • Autini
        • Sophenia
        • Andeluna
        • Salentein

                40

                Tunuyán
        Lurton •
    94
    Flecha de los Arches •
        Monteviejo •   Vista Flores
    Clos de los Siete •   92
    Tikal Vineyard •   • Altoudro
    La Consulta •   • San Carlos
        • Finca La Celia
        • O. Fournier

                40

MENDOZA

Mendoza City
    • Godoy Cruz
        • Maipú
    • Luján • Junin
Tupungato •   • Rivadavia

    • Tunuyán

    • San Carlos

N

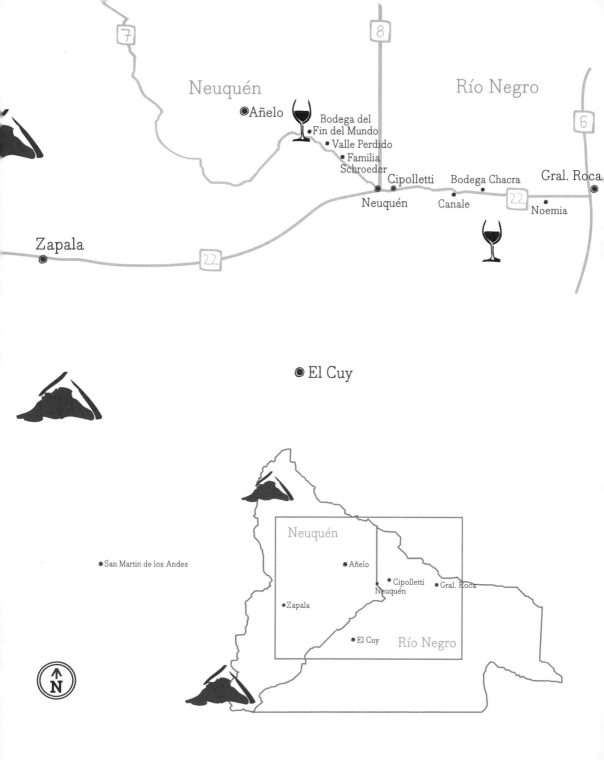

PATAGONIA, NEUQUÉN, AND RÍO NEGRO

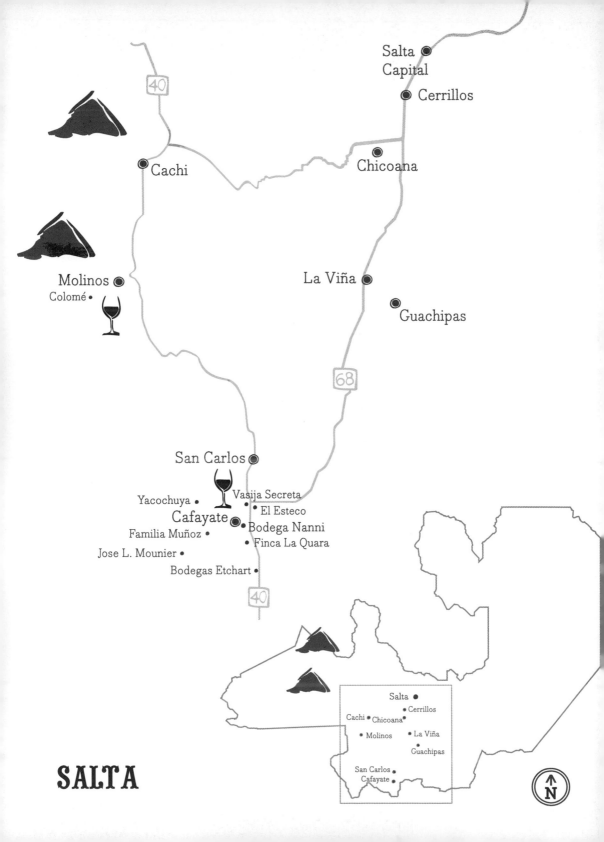

Salta
Capital ◉

◉ Cerrillos

40

◉ Chicoana

◉ Cachi

◉ Molinos
Colomé ·

◉ La Viña

◉ Guachipas

68

San Carlos ◉

Yacochuya ·   · Vasija Secreta
Cafayate ·   · El Esteco
· · Bodega Nanni
Familia Muñoz · · Finca La Quara
Jose L. Mounier ·
Bodegas Etchart ·

40

SALTA

Salta ·
Cachi · · Chicoana   · Cerrillos
· Molinos   · La Viña
· Guachipas
San Carlos ·
Cafayate ·

↑
N

ACKNOWLEDGEMENTS

Thanks to everyone who participated in this book.

– Laura Catena

A

Achaval, Santiago, 89, 94

Achaval-Ferrer, 89, 94, 213

Adrianna Vineyard, 123, 125

Agrelo, 98, 99, 101

Alamos, 156

Alfajores de maizena, 43, 192–93

Almacén del Sur, 78, 211

Almacén de Uco, 134, 215

Almonds, caramelized, 187

Alta Vista, 79, 211

Altocedro, 215

Altos las Hormigas, 79, 83, 211

Andeluna, 114, 215

Antigal, 117

Antonini, Alberto, 30, 80, 83–84

Argentina. *See also individual
   provinces and cities*

   history of, 19–20, 41

   immigration to, 38, 40–42

   instability of, 166–67

   Native peoples of, 41–42, 151

   population of, 38, 166

   size of, 38

   travel tips for, 167–68

   wine-growing provinces of,
      18–19, 166

   wine itinerary for, 168, 170

Argento, 68

Asado, 43, 48, 51, 170

Astrid y Gaston, 170, 218

Ayala, Rodrigo, 186

Azafrán, 210

B

Baily, Samuel, 40

Balbo, Susana, 33, 99

Barbecue. *See Asado*

Barbera, 21

Bar 878, 171, 218

Bargaining, 167

Bariloche, 140

Barraud, Luis, 89, 90

Beef

   Argentine, 36–37, 43

   carbonada, 178–79

   empanadas salteñas, 174–77

   milanesas, 181–82

   ojo de bife, 46

   ordering steak, 167–68

   rib-eye steak with chimichurri
      and Patagonian potatoes,
      183, 185

Belasco de Baquedano, 101, 214

Bella Vista Vineyard, 94

Benegas, 79

Bereber, 170, 218

Berry chutney, 186–87

Bianchieri, Anne-Caroline, 134

Biodynamic farming, 200

Bistro M, 210

Bodega, definition of, 200

Bonarda, 21, 67, 74–75, 200

Bonnie, Alfred, 17

Bórmida, Eliana, 116–17

Buenos Aires

    culinary influence of, 36

    history of, 19–20, 56

    population of, 166

    restaurants and bars in, 170–71

Buscema, Fernando, 93–94, 158

Bustos, Lucas, 89, 178

C

Cabaña Las Lilas, 37, 168, 170, 218

Cabernet Sauvignon, 21, 26, 27

Cafayate, 150, 151–52, 155

Café Tortoni, 171, 218

Calchaquí Valley, 152

Canavan, Tom, 155

Carbonada, 43, 178–79

Cardones, Parque Nacional
    de los, 152

CARO, Bodegas, 33, 62–63, 210

Casa Antucura, 134, 215

Casa Argento, 211

Casa Cruz, 170, 218

Castillo, Pedro, 55

Catamarca, 166

Catena, Domingo, 29, 40, 68, 99

Catena, Elena, 104, 105, 181, 193

Catena, Ernesto, 105, 131, 136–37

Catena, Joanna, 137

Catena, Nicola, 27, 31, 38, 40, 41, 67

Catena, Nicolás, 11, 16–18, 22–23,
    28–30, 31–33, 90–91, 104, 117–18

Catena, Vincenzo and María, 40

Catena Zapata, Bodega, 31, 42, 99,
    101, 103–5, 107, 122, 123, 125, 214

Cavas Wine Lodge, 89, 168, 197, 214

Chacra, 143, 144, 146–47, 216

Chacras de Coria, 78, 80

Charbonneau, 75

Chardonnay, 21, 109, 123

Chimeno, Vanina, 189

Chimichurri, 45, 183, 185

Choripán, 45

Chorizo, 45

Chuit, Cecilia Diaz, 197

Chutney, berry, 186–87

Cinzano, Noemi, 143, 144, 146

Cipresso, Roberto, 89, 94

Clos de los Siete, 33, 129, 131, 133,
    134, 215

Cobos, 33, 89, 90, 213

Coconut

    alfajores de maizena, 192–93

    toasting, 193

Colomé Winery, 150, 161–62, 174, 195, 217

Congo Bar, 171, 218

Cookies

    alfajores de maizena, 192–93

Corbeau, 75

Corn

    carbonada, 178–79

Crepes with dulce de leche, 189–91

Criolla, 20, 21, 56, 129, 200

Criolla Chica, 156

Crios, 156

Cuvée, 200

D

Dagueneau, Didier, 107

Darwin, Charles, 71

Davalos, Jaime, 158

Desserts

    alfajores de maizena, 192–93

    helado de Torrontés, 195

    quince, 197

Dinosaurs, 143

Directions, asking for, 167

Dolcetto, 75

Dolium, 101, 117, 214

Domaine, 200

Dominio del Plata, 33, 99, 214

Doña Paula, 60, 101, 214

Don Bosco School of Enology, 16, 33

Don Mario, 37, 210

Drinking, 167

Dufllet, Philip, 131

Dulce de batata, 45

Dulce de leche, 45, 189, 191

    alfajores de maizena, 192–93

    crepes with, 189–91

Dulce de membrillo, 45

E

Eco de los Andes, 130

El Carrizal, 68

El Cielo, 136, 215

El Esteco, 155, 217

El Green Bamboo, 170, 218

Elia, Pablo Sánchez, 105

El Ilo, 113–14

El Manzano Histórico, 128, 130

Emberson, Carl, 57

Empanadas, 45

    salteñas, 174–77

English, Todd, 43

Enrique Foster, 79, 211

Ernesto Catena Vineyards, 216

Escorihuela Gascón, 28, 47, 60,
   62, 210

Esmeralda, Bodegas, 28, 68, 90, 105

Etchart, 155, 156, 157, 158, 217

Etchart, Arnaldo, 157, 158

Etchart, Marcos, 157

Eugenio Bustos, 131

F

Fabre, Diane and Hervé Joyaux, 143

Fabre Montmayou, 79, 143, 211

Faena Hotel, 171, 220

Familia Bianchi, 166

Familia Roca, 166

Familia Schroeder, 141, 143, 216

Familia Zuccardi, 74, 211

Felix Lavaque, 155, 156, 157, 217

Fiesta de la Vendimia, 57

Fiesta del Tomate, 129

Fiesta Nacional del Oregano, 129

Finca Alegria, 68

Finca La Anita, 214

Finca las Nubes, 156–57

Finca Sophenia, 114, 116, 117, 215

Fin del Mundo, Bodega del, 134, 141,
   143, 216

Flechas de los Andes, 131, 215

Flichman, 117

Foster, Enrique, 79

Francesco Ristorante, 210

François Lurton, 129, 216

Fruhinshole, Adolfo, 28

G

Gaja, Angelo, 31

Galante, José, 29, 90

Galtieri, Jim, 62

Gascón, Don Miguel, 27, 60, 62

Gauchito Gil, 72–73

Gauchos, 41, 71–73

Gayan, Marina, 33

Grafted vines, 107, 109

Gran Bar Danzon, 171, 218

Grands cru, 201

Guaraníes, 42

H

Hail, 68, 71

Halsrick, Miguel, 38, 91–92

Hang time, 201

Helado de Torrontés, 195

Herbrard, Jacques, 26

Hess, Donald, 30, 150, 152, 161–62

Hess, Ursula, 150, 161–62, 174, 195

Higounet, Charles, 26

Hobbs, Paul, 17, 30, 89, 90–91

Hotel rates, 167

Huarpe Indians, 19, 41, 56

Humberto Canale, 143, 144, 216

Humitas, 45

I

Ice cream

    helado de Torrontés, 195

Il Matterello, 170, 218

Ilo Restaurant Tupungato, 215

Immigration, 38, 40–42

Incas, 19, 151

Incisa della Rocchetta, Mario, 146

Incisa della Rocchetta, Piero, 143–44,
    146–47

Infinitus, 143

Instituto Nacional de
    Vitivinicultura, 21

Itinerary, suggested, 168, 170

J

Jackson, Jess, 41

Johnson, Hugh, 26

Johnson, Randle, 161

José L. Mounier, Bodega, 155, 156, 217

K

Kaiken, 60

Kemp, Sarah, 31

Kiss, as greeting, 167

L

La Barra, 37, 210

La Boca, 168

Laborde, 74

La Bourgogne, 78, 171, 211, 218

La Brigada, 37, 170, 219

La Caballeriza, 170, 219

La Cabaña, 170, 219

La Cabrera, 170, 219

La Consulta, 136

La Dorita, 37, 219

Lagarde, 33, 79, 212

Langes, Gernot, 91

La Posada del Jamón, 134, 216

La Rioja, 166

La Rural, Bodega, 20, 79, 80

La Rural Wine Museum, 80, 212

Las Cañitas, 219

Lavaque, 155, 156, 157, 166, 217

La Viruta, 219

Lay, H. Ward, 114

Libelula, 170, 219

Llao Llao Hotel, 37, 186, 216

Lomito, 45

Lomo, 45

Lopez, Bodegas, 79

Luca Winery, 33, 129

Luigi Bosca, 79, 212

Luján de Cuyo

    Agrelo and Ugarteche, 98, 99, 101

    northern, 78, 79

    Perdriel, 88, 89

Luka, Roberto, 116

Lurton, François, 129

Lurton, Jacques, 17, 129

Lurton, Pierre, 89

M

Maceration, 201

Maipú, 78–80

Malbec

    characteristics of, 23, 134, 201

    history of, 20, 21, 24, 26–31, 201

    own-rooted vines and, 109

    popularity of, 23, 30

    quality and, 28–30

Mallmann, Francis, 37, 47, 62, 168, 183, 189

Maps, 222–24

Marchevski, Pedro, 29, 99

Marchiori, Andrea, 33, 89, 90

Masi Passo Doble, 116

Masi Tupungato, 116

Masters of Food and Wine event, 57

Mate, 45–46

Mayans, 105, 137

Mayor Drummond, 79, 80

Melezca, 93–94

Melipal, 83, 89, 213

Mendel, 33, 79, 85, 212

Mendoza, Angel, 23

Mendoza, Garcia Hurtado de, 55

Mendoza City

    acequias of, 59

    attractions of, 54, 55

    celebrations of, 57

    climate of, 54

    food in, 54

    history of, 55–57, 59

    plazas of, 59–60

    population of, 56–57

    transportation to, 54

    trees of, 59

    wine and, 54, 60, 62–63

Mendoza Province

    appellations in, 79

    climate of, 10, 68, 71, 121–22

    culinary revolution in, 36

    eastern, 66–68, 71

    high-altitude desert viticulture in, 117–18

    history of, 16, 19–20, 27, 55–57

    immigration to, 38, 60

irrigation in, 122

local specialties of, 37

location of, 10

Luján de Cuyo, 78, 79, 88, 89, 98, 99, 101

map, 222

Primera Zona, 78–80

soils of, 10–11, 118, 121

Uco Valley, 112–14, 128–31, 134, 136

wine production by, 18, 56, 57, 83

Meredith, Carole, 156

Merlot, 21, 140

Michel Torino, 152, 156

Milanesas, 46, 181–82

Minerality, 202

Minga, 170, 219

Molinos, 152

Mondavi, Robert, 17, 23, 31

Mondovino (film), 133, 158

Money, counterfeit, 167

Monteviejo, 33, 131, 215

Moscato d'Asti, 21

Mota, Raúl de la, 84

Mota, Roberto de la, 26, 33, 84–85

Mounier, José Luis, 156–57

Mouthfeel, 202

Muscat of Alexandria, 156

N

Nakbé, 137

Napoli, María, 38, 40

National School of Agronomy, 24

Navarro Correas, 117

Négociant, 202

Neuquén, 140–41, 143, 223

Nicolás Catena, Bodegas y Viñedos, 27

Nieto Senetiner, 79, 83, 212

Noemia Winery, 143, 144, 146, 217

Norton, 38, 89, 91, 117, 213

Norton, Edward, 38, 91

Nose, 202

Nossiter, Jonathan, 133

NQN, 85, 141, 217

O

O. Fournier, 116, 117, 131, 134, 216

O'Higgins, Bernardo, 60

Ojo de bife, 46

Old vines, 202

Ortega, José Manuel, 30, 131

Ortega, Natalia, 134

Osaka, 170, 219

Oviedo, 171, 219

Own-rooted vines, 107, 109, 203

Oxidative style, 155, 203

P

Pacha, 171, 219

Pagli, Attilio, 17

Paolo, Mariano di, 47, 114

Paris, Judgment of, 28

Parker, Robert, Jr., 30, 31, 84

Park Hyatt

    Mendoza, 59, 210

    Palacio Duhau, 220

Parrals, 73–74, 203

Parrilla, 46

Pascual Toso, Bodegas y Viñedos, 79, 211

Patagonia

    climate of, 140, 141, 143

    dinosaurs in, 143

    local specialties of, 37, 140

    map, 223

    size of, 141

    transportation to, 140

    wines of, 140, 141

Patagonia Sur, 47, 168, 220

Patios de Cafayate, 152, 217

Paulucci, Angel, 21

Pedro Giménez, 20–21

Perdriel, 88, 89

Péré-Vergé, Catherine, 33, 131

Perinetti, Estela, 33, 62, 63

Pescarmona, Sofia, 33

Petit Verdot, 67–68

Peynaud, Émile, 84

Phylloxera, 107, 203

Pini, Egisto, 74

Pinot Blanco, 21

Pinot Noir, 123, 140, 146–47

Pisoni, Gary, 107

Plaza Grill at the Marriott Plaza Hotel, 170, 220

Potatoes

    carbonada, 178–79

    Patagonian, 183, 185

Pouget, Michel Aimé, 20, 24, 201

Presilla, Maricel, 10

Primera Zona, 78–80

Protective style, 155, 203

Pulenta, Antonio, 16, 101

Pulenta, Carlos, 79

Pulenta, Eduardo, 101

Pulenta Estate, 101, 117, 214

Q

Quince

    dessert, 197

    dulce de membrillo, 45

Quinta Nacional, 16, 20, 24

Quiroga, Facundo, 24

R

Reginato, Luis, 129, 130

Renacer, 60, 83, 213

Restaurante 1884, 47, 62, 189, 210

Río Negro, 140–41, 143, 223

Ripe style, 203

Rivadavia, 74, 75

Robinson, Jancis, 16, 24

Roca, Julio Argentino, 41

Rolland, Michel, 30, 33, 41, 129, 133–34, 157, 158

Rothschild, Eric de, 62, 63

Ruca Malen, 89, 213

Ruseler, Sonia, 68

Rutini, Rodolfo Reina, 20, 80

Rutini Tupungato, 114, 117

S

Salentein, 114, 116–17, 215

Salentein Posada, 215

Salin, Christophe, 62

Salta

    attractions of, 150, 151–52

    climate of, 150

    history of, 56

    local specialties of, 37, 150

    map, 224

    transportation to, 150

    wines of, 150, 152, 155–58, 161–62

San Carlos, 18, 128–30

San Juan, 166

San Martín, José de, 59–60, 128, 130

San Martín de Los Andes, 140, 141

San Patricio del Chañar, 140, 141

San Pedro de Yacochuya, 155, 156, 157, 217

San Rafael, 166

Sarmiento, Domingo Faustino, 24

Sassicaia, 146, 147

Sejanovich, Alejandro, 29, 101, 122, 123

Semillon, 21

Señor Tango, 171, 220

Séptima, 101, 117, 214

Seven Fires (Mallmann), 47

Sielecki, Annabelle, 33, 85

Smith, David, 68

Stainless-steel tanks, 204

Stone, Larry, 31

Suarez, Leopoldo, 24

Sucre, 168, 170, 220

Sweet potatoes

    carbonada, 178–79

    dulce de batata, 45

    venison with berry chutney, caramelized almonds, and, 186–88

Syrah, 21, 67

T

Tango, 171, 220

Tannins, 204

Tapiz, 101, 214

Tegui, 170, 220

Tempranillo, 21, 67

Terrazas de Los Andes, 89, 213

Terroir, 18, 107, 204

Tête de cuvée, 204

Tikal Vineyard, 131, 136–37

Tilia, 156

Tipicity, 204

Tipping, 168

Tomo I, 170, 220

Torrontés, 21, 155–57, 204

Trapiche, 23, 79, 212

Travel tips, 167–68

Trivento, 60, 79, 212

Trocca, Fernando, 168

Tunuyán, 128–30, 134

Tupungato, 112–14, 116

U

Uco Valley, 112–14, 128–31, 134, 136

Ugarteche, 98, 99, 101

Ungrafted vines. *See* Own-rooted vines

Urban, 134

V

Varietal, definition of, 204

Venison with berry chutney, sweet potatoes, and caramelized almonds, 186–88

Verdot, 20

Vigil, Alejandro, 103–4

Vinding-Diers, Hans, 143, 144, 146

Vines of Mendoza Tasting Room, 210

Vinify, definition of, 204

Vino patero, 20

Viola, Julio, 143

Vista Flores, 131

Vistalba, Bodega, 79, 80, 117, 211

W

Wines, Argentine. *See also individual varietals and wineries*

average consumption of, 22

exporting, 22–23, 30

history of, 16–17, 19–23

provinces producing, 18–19, 166

terroir and, 18

varietals of, 20–21

Wines of Argentina (wine exports association), 33

Women winemakers, 33

Y

Yacochuya, 133, 134

Yanzon, Mario, 116–17

Yerba mate, 45–46

Z

Zuccardi, José Alberto, 74, 75

Zumel, Emilio, 38